get
Spun

get Spun

The Step-by-Step Guide to Spinning Art Yarns

Symeon North

INTERWEAVE.
interweavestore.com

EDITOR
Anne Merrow

TECHNICAL EDITOR
Abby Franquemont

PHOTOGRAPHY
Joe Coca

PHOTO STYLING AND PROCESS PHOTOGRAPHY
Ann Sabin Swanson

COVER AND INTERIOR DESIGN
Connie Poole

PRODUCTION
Katherine Jackson

Interweave Press LLC
201 East Fourth Street
Loveland, CO 80537-5655 USA
interweavestore.com

Printed in China by C&C Offset.

Library of Congress Cataloging-in-Publication Data

North, Symeon.
 Get spun : the step-by-step guide to spinning art yarns /
Symeon North.
    p. cm.
 Includes bibliographical references and index.
 ISBN 978-1-59668-064-7
 1. Hand spinning. 2. Dyes and dyeing--Textile fibers.
 3. Spun yarns.
 I. Title.
 TT847.N67 2010
 746.1'2--dc22
                          2009045236

10 9 8 7 6 5 4 3 2 1

"The wheel is turning and you can't slow down . . .
Every time that wheel turn round, bound to cover just a little more ground "
—Robert Hunter, "The Wheel"

For my grandmother, who wasn't a very good knitter; but refused to let that fact stop her.
Thanks for teaching me (much) more than how to knit.

For all of those who have gone before me, and for those who will come after me.

acknowledgments

It is amazing that this book is finally finished! It has survived four computers, a cross-country move, and about nineteen nervous breakdowns.

I would like to thank everyone who stood by me and offered support and encouragement during this process, both in three dimensions and online. I couldn't have done any of it without your rooting me on.

Anne Merrow, my wonderful editor, listened and poked and went above and beyond for me.

Abby Franquemont, the technical editor goddess with a lifetime of spinning experience behind her, gave her all.

Ann Swanson made my first photo shoot so much fun (and beautiful!).

Tricia Waddell and everyone at Interweave, thanks for believing in this project.

Jillian Moreno put this bug in my ear in the first place. (There were times I questioned the sanity of this idea.)

Last but not least, my dear family. Now I hope you all realize when Mama says she has to work, she really means it. Thank you, Matt, Izabella, and Cyrus for all the helping hands, love, encouragement, and picking up my slack. I love you people!

contents

what makes
an art yarn?

Art n. skill; human skill as opposed to nature; skill applied to music, painting, poetry, etc.; any one of the subjects of this skill; system of rules; profession or craft.

Yarn n. spun thread of fiber prepared for weaving, knitting, etc.

There we have it, according to Webster: the definition of an "art yarn." Humans have been struggling to define art since we started to create, and the subjective nature of art makes it all the more difficult to reduce to a simple definition. Perhaps that is why many of us are drawn to the creative process.

What makes a yarn an art yarn and not simply a novelty yarn? Artistry and intention, of course. When you set out to create yarn that is an object of beauty, then you have an art yarn—even if that yarn is a gray cobweb-weight three-ply. Art, like beauty, is in the eye of the beholder.

An art yarn is much like a painting. The details—each fiber, every ply—are like brushstrokes. And like trained artists, we must first learn the principles of realism before we can go surreal. Art yarn reflects the skill set from which it was created. Spinning, just like painting, will only get better with more practice.

This book covers some of the many "hows" in art yarn spinning, and with some luck, a few "whys." Beginning with choosing and preparing your materials and continuing through drafting and plying, every choice you make in spinning can bring the finished yarn closer to the expression of your personal and artistic ideas.

tools & materials

Art yarns can incorporate many different kinds of fiber, but the basic materials you'll need to get started are relatively simple and easy to obtain. With just some wool and a spinning wheel you can begin to create exciting and adventurous yarns, but some additional equipment and a range of materials will open up a whole new world of possibilities.

Tools

Many of the tools used for spinning art yarns are identical to those used for spinning any other yarn. You may use some of the tools a bit differently, but the basics are the same. Some spinners prefer a collection of spinning wheels and tools with different specialties. The key to choosing the right equipment is to find what works best for you. Don't be afraid to experiment or try other equipment, even if you ultimately stick with what you have because it works.

spinning wheel

A spinning wheel with a large orifice may be the most specialized item I use for spinning art yarns, and it is the most vital piece in my collection of gadgets. Find a wheel that you are comfortable with. Otherwise, it will sit alone, gathering dust. I spin much of my yarn on a rather large, clunky Woolhouse "bulky spinner" that was made in the 1970s. The orifice is about 1 inch (2.5 cm) wide, plenty big for my needs, and the bobbin can hold about a pound (454 g) of fiber. Although this particular wheel is no longer in production, bulky spinners can often be found for sale among used spinning wheels. Ashford currently produces a Country Spinner with a 7/8-inch (2.2 cm) orifice and very large bobbins.

My first wheel, which I still use, is an Ashford Traditional, a workhorse of a wheel. It's good for spinning just about anything and easily expandable with a bulky flyer or quill attachment (see below). Other manufacturers also offer accessories useful for spinning bulky yarns; they generally have low drive ratios (10:1 or less), making it easier to spin thicker yarns. When you're spinning art yarns, especially at the beginning, you may be able to add twist faster than you can draft, and a lower ratio may help your hands keep up with the twist.

In addition to a larger orifice, wheels used for spinning art yarns may need a different range of ratios than you do for classic yarns. Lendrum flyers have the whorls attached directly to the flyer, and the larger orifice is paired with larger whorls. If the flyer and the whorl are separate, as for the Schacht bulky flyer, you can choose to pair a fast or slow ratio with the large orifice and bobbin.

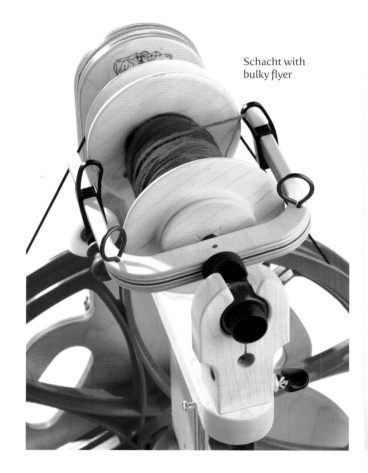

Schacht with bulky flyer

It is possible to spin art yarns with a quill or spindle wheel (which uses a pointed shaft to store and spin yarn). The quill or spindle is most often seen on an old-fashioned great wheel or a charkha used for spinning cotton; it is generally used to produce thin high-twist yarns. However, it has no orifice, giving it a huge advantage for spinning larger yarns—there is no limit to the diameter of the yarn! With patience and practice, you could easily spin a low-twist yarn on it.

Unless you have a quill or an orifice you can fit your fingers into, you will also need an **orifice hook**. They range from a bent paper clip to a piece of wire with a fancy lampworked glass or carved wood handle. Anything that can make its way into and through the orifice, grab the leader or yarn smoothly, and draw it back through will work fine. You'll need some form of **lazy kate** to hold bobbins of yarn for plying.

Lendrum with
bulky flyer

What about spindles?

I won't be discussing spindles here, because I can't produce the types of yarn I want on them. This isn't to say it can't be done—it can. Shortly after an article I wrote about coiled yarns appeared in *Knitty* magazine, readers sent me pictures of coiled yarns they'd made on spindles. Still, I'd rather tell you about the techniques that have worked for me than ones I haven't used successfully.

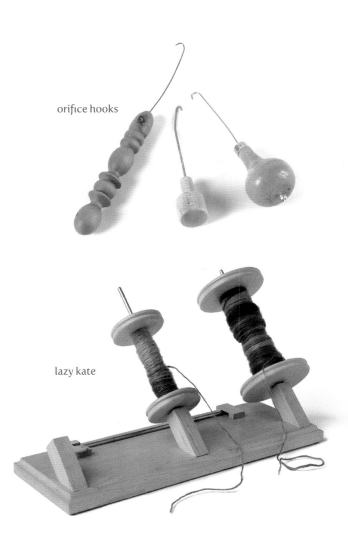

orifice hooks

lazy kate

drumcarder

brush

doffer

drumcarder

Another indispensable piece of equipment is my drumcarder. For the amount of yarn I like to produce when I create blends, handcards are out of the question. There are many choices of carders. Although some might splurge on a large or an electric drumcarder to save time, I find a Louet Junior large enough to make whatever I want to create.

other tools

There is a plethora of other gadgets you can acquire that may be helpful in your process. A **sett gauge** is a small tool for measuring wraps per inch (wpi; see page 59). Because mine is perpetually lost, I use a **ruler** for the task. A **protractor** can be handy for measuring twists per inch (tpi) or angle of twist (see page 60). A precise **scale** helps measure materials for blending and find the yards per pound.

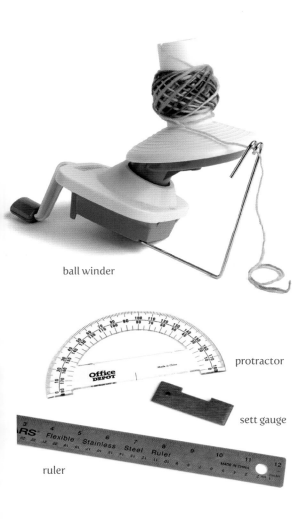

ball winder

protractor

sett gauge

ruler

skeiner

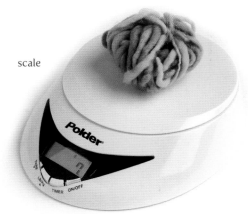

scale

I use a **ball winder** to make center-pull balls for some kinds of art yarns. And a niddy-noddy or swift will do, but I prefer a yarn reel or **skeiner** to wind skeins of yarn off the bobbin for finishing.

That's it! You may find other tools that you prefer, and you will need dedicated (though not very specialized) equipment if you'd like to venture into dyeing (see page 20). But for the most part, you can start spinning art yarns with equipment you already own or can borrow.

wool locks

wool batt

wool top

Materials

One of the first big differences between spinning art yarn and traditional yarn is the range of materials you use. Art yarn can incorporate all of the fibers that traditional yarn does—wool, silks, plant fibers, synthetic fibers—but plastic bags, recycled fabric, pom-poms, and the like definitely push the spinning envelope. Combining classic and funky elements in your own way makes a yarn uniquely your own.

wool

Wool and hair are protein fibers from animals. They can be dyed readily with acid dyes. Wool is incredibly versatile and is by far the most common material for spinning yarns, art and otherwise. Wool refers to fiber from sheep, but other animal fibers are spinning staples, too. They can range from ultra-fine, such as bison down, to long and soft, such as alpaca, to glossy and curly, such as mohair. (See page 22 for information on dyeing wool and protein fibers.)

One property that makes wool especially useful to art yarn spinners is the fact that it can felt. Even if you're not planning to make a completely fulled or felted yarn, the cuticle of wool and hair will help it grab other elements in the yarn, integrating them and making them structurally sound. (For more on this, see Finishing Yarn, page 62.)

Wool is available in a variety of preparations: **locks** are loose clumps of wool in the same formation they came off the sheep, roving and **batts** are carded to be partly aligned, and **top** has been combed to remove shorter fibers and arrange the wool very evenly. I use a lot of dyed locks in my work for added texture and color.

silk top

sari silk

silk cocoons

silk noil

silk

The form of silk most common to spinners is probably **silk top**, which can be either bombyx (cultivated) or tussah (wild). The fibers in silk top can be extremely long. There are other ways you can buy this versatile fiber.

Recycled **sari silk** is amazingly fun and adds a special spunk to yarns. This fiber is made up of very fine strands of silk thread that are cut away in the process of making silk saris; most of the available recycled sari silk is stuff that might literally be thrown away if it weren't used for spinning. Because it was once part of other cloth, it comes in a huge range of colors, all mixed together.

Silk noil is another form of reclaimed silk, generally the leftover short fibers from reeling or carding silk. It can be wonderfully soft and colorful, and silk noil adds texture to tweedy yarns.

Silk cocoons are a wonderful add-in; they take acid dyes beautifully and provide an instant "wow" factor. The silk cocoons I use are the discarded houses of silk worms; the hole in the top is where the worm chewed its way out. This type of silk is often called "vegetarian silk" because the worms do not die in the harvesting process as they do in many other forms.

hemp

Hemp (like the more common linen) is a long, strong plant fiber that has been important to textile makers since the very beginning. Hemp can't be grown legally in the United States because it is a member of the Cannabis family, although hemp grown for fiber doesn't contain the chemical that would make it intoxicating. It is imported as fiber. Hemp and other plant fibers are made of cellulose; they must be dyed with fiber-reactive dyes (see page 34).

hemp

glitz

There are many synthetic fibers that can add sparkle to your yarns. They may be sold as Angelina, Firestar, or simply glitz. A little bit can go a long way, so I use this mostly in blends.

fabric, plastic bags, and other "unspinnables"

Part of the fun of making art yarns is finding and incorporating materials that no one but you might think of as part of a yarn. I love spinning **fabric** and trim finds from outgrown clothes or expeditions to thrift stores. The **plastic bags** that seem to multiply when my back is turned can add a fun textural element to yarn. Look around for yourself!

glitz

fabric

plastic bags

above left: metallic sewing thread
above right: crochet cotton

thread, elastic, and yarn

Although I love to have a hand in creating most of the elements in my yarn, there are times when purchased thread, elastic, or yarn is just what the project calls for. Commercial **threads** can add shine and strength, and their even diameter can be perfect for stringing beads and other elements. **Elastic thread** can produce really exciting effects, such as super-springy yarns. Serger thread, **crochet cotton**, and even your own already-spun yarn come in handy as elements in art yarns.

miscellany

From plain beads to **pom-poms**, ribbons to **hardware**, the sky's the limit when it comes to adding fun elements to your yarn. Raid your bead stash, button box, or office supply drawer. Soon you'll be looking at all kinds of items with new eyes, imagining them as part of your next art yarn.

elastic thread

hardware

mixed glass beads

pom-poms

dye fiber & yarn

Color color COLOR! Bold and bright or soft and subtle, color is what makes or breaks a yarn for me. We each have our own way with color; it is just a matter of exploring and making it work in our favor. Without delving into the rich world of color theory, we will go over the basics, which will serve as a jumping-off point for your own explorations of color. Color is a phenomenal way to inject personality, emotion, and spirit into your fiber.

Dyeing Protein Fibers

We will start with protein fibers such as wool and silk, because I have found them to be the simplest and most forgiving (and my favorites) to dye. Whether you are dyeing locks, prepared wool top, silk, or yarn, the process is pretty much the same. For protein fibers such as silk and wool, look for acid dyes. I have experimented with an array of dye brands and types, and my absolute favorites come from Jacquard because of the price and the wide color spectrum.

You're probably eager to get dyeing, but a little effort in good preparation makes a huge difference in the quality of your results. Both the dye and the fiber need some special treatment before they can meet.

you will need:

* Protein fiber
* Water
* Acid dye (either professional or food-grade)
* Acid (usually vinegar or citric-acid crystals)
* Heat source
* Heatproof container

Before dyeing, your fibers need to be soaked in warm water until they are thoroughly saturated. The looser your fibers, the less time it will take—roughly 15 minutes for loose locks and up to an hour or more for high-twist yarn. After soaking is complete, gently remove the fibers and strain the excess water. Handle the fibers as little as possible, because they are more apt to nep (break, snarl, and pill) and felt while warm and wet. A colander works well to hold and drain your fibers.

While the fibers are draining, it is a good time to prepare the dye mixture. Prepare your dye by creating a slurry of dye powder and water that has come to a boil. Place your dye in a heatproof container (such as a recycled glass jar) and slowly add a few tablespoons of the boiled water, just enough so you can thoroughly mix all of the dye powder with water. (Consult the directions from the dye manufacturer or a reference like *Color in Spinning* by Deb Menz or *The Dyer's Companion* by Dagmar Klos for exact proportions of dye, water, and fiber.)

If you are using citric-acid crystals, add them when your dye slurry is made, then add the rest of your hot water. (Citric acid is often less expensive than vinegar and it lacks the strong odor.) If you are using white vinegar for your acid, add the remaining water and vinegar together.

1. Soak the fiber or yarn in warm water.

2. Strain the water from your fiber very gently.

Dye Safety

When my children were very young, I used food and cake dyes exclusively for dyeing because I found the word "acid" intimidating. Truth be told, food-grade dyes are also acid dyes.

Although professional synthetic dyes are relatively safe, it is imperative to use a dust mask and dye in a well-ventilated room when working with a powder. (This rule also goes for drink mixes and other food-grade powder dyes.) Pots, baking sheets, slow cookers, spoons, containers, and other utensils that contain dye or otherwise come into direct contact with it should be set aside for dyeing only and never see food again.

Gloves are also necessary—who likes to go out into the non-fiber world with purple hands and nails? The molecules of the dye are too large to get into your body through the pores on your skin, but it is strongly suggested that you don gloves if you have any cuts or scrapes. This is not just for safety reasons; getting acid or salt in there will hurt! (Think lemon juice.) Gloves give a small amount (a very small amount!) of thermal protection when you are handling liquids while they are still hot. Gloves will also help protect your fiber from your hands, especially if you are prone to "garden hands" like I am—rough hands can promote felting or snags, especially when working with a fine fiber such as silk.

kettle dyeing

Kettle dyeing (also known as immersion dyeing) produces subtle variations of color. With kettle dyeing, we take full advantage of the bleeding and blending of similar colors. The technique is most useful for achieving a slightly variegated fiber within the same color family, such as blues to greens, or for solid colors.

you will need:

* Presoaked protein fiber
* Additional vinegar or other acidifier
* Water
* Slow cooker or other heat source and container
* Prepared dye stock

Place the fibers to be dyed in a warm bath of acid and water in a slow cooker or other pot. Use about 1 part acid (white vinegar or dissolved citric-acid crystals) to 10 parts water. The more water in the pot, the more the dye will bleed and blend. To dye a solid tone, it is best to cover the fiber completely with water and then some, which will allow the fibers to "swim" in the dye bath. Gently pour your mixed dye over the submerged fibers.

Set the slow cooker on medium or place the pot on a burner on very low heat; the liquid shouldn't boil, so keep it between 160° and 190°F (71° and 88°C). Cover the pot and let it cook until all the dye has been exhausted, or taken up into the fibers. (You will know the dye has been exhausted when there is no more color in the dyebath—it should look clear or nearly so.) Some colors take more time to exhaust, and others may not exhaust completely—experiment until you feel comfortable with all different kinds. Remember to allow the fiber to cool to room temperature before removing it from the pot and straining it. Gently rinse the fiber to remove the vinegar or other acid and allow it to dry.

1. Place the fiber in a pot with enough water-vinegar mixture to cover the fiber.

2. Pour the dye over the fibers.

3. Applying the dye a little unevenly will create a slightly mottled look instead of a solid.

multicolored kettle dyeing

You can create a hybrid between kettle dyeing and hand-painting by dyeing your fiber or yarn layer by layer in a slow cooker or other vessel. This method allows you to place several colors with a little more precision than kettle dyeing does.

you will need:

* Presoaked protein fiber or yarn
* Prepared dye stock
* Slow cooker or other container and heat source

Prepare the fiber (or yarn) the same way that you would for kettle dyeing but stop before arranging the fiber or yarn and pouring on the water. Instead of immersing the fibers in the acid/water mixture, add the liquid to the dye mixtures. Arrange one layer of fiber in the pot. Carefully apply one color of dye over a designated area of fiber colors by pouring, sponging, painting with a brush, or using a dye syringe. Each area should remain consistent for every layer of fiber.

Apply the second color in the same fashion, leaving an area undyed to absorb any bleeding. (Your bottom layer will be your darkest layer. To compensate, try leaving more white space on that layer and reducing the white areas near the top.) Repeat for a third (and fourth, or more) color. Once the first layer has had all dye applied, add another layer of undyed fibers. Apply your second (and subsequent) layers of dye in the same area of the pot where you poured the dye for the first layer.

Turn your slow cooker on medium heat, put the lid on, and cook until all the dye has been exhausted. Allow the fiber to cool to room temperature, then remove it from the pot and strain it in a colander. Rinse gently and allow to dry.

MULTICOLORED KETTLE DYEING

1. Arrange one layer of fiber in the slow cooker.

2. Carefully apply the first color of dye.

3. Add one or more additional colors on the first layer.

4. Add another layer of undyed fibers.

5. Pour dye over the next layer, keeping the colors in the same area as on the first layer.

6. Cover the fiber and heat until the dye is absorbed.

7. After the dyebath has cooled, remove the fiber.

8. Drain the dyed fiber in a colander before rinsing and drying it.

handpainting

Adding color at the exact spot where you want it makes irresistible yarn and fiber, and the kind of control that you can maintain makes this a wonderful opportunity for artistic expression.

Handpainting can be as simple or complex as you want to get. You can use silk painting brushes, sponge paintbrushes, or dye syringes (special syringes with no needle, sometimes sold in veterinary supply stores for administering medicine orally). I often use regular household sponges cut into quarters.

you will need:

* Presoaked fiber or yarn
* Plastic wrap
* Water/vinegar mixture
* Prepared dye stock
* Dye applicators (syringes, sponges, or brushes)
* Slow cooker and colander or other oven-safe container and heat source

handpainted wool top

HANDPAINTING FIBER One of the advantages of hand-painting fiber is the ability to keep colors more distinct and less blended. Once your fibers are completely drained of excess water, you can arrange them. Cover your surface in newspapers and lay the fiber out in manageable sections on plastic wrap. ("Manageable sections" is relative; it really depends on exactly how much space you can spare.) I prefer to lay mine out in 2-foot (61 cm) sections for shorter color repeats and easier handling.

To preserve the integrity of the individual colors, add the 10:1 water-acid mixture to your dye mixture instead of submerging the fiber in it. Use the dye when the mixture is still warm to help the dyes strike instantly. Some dyers also add acid to the initial soaking water or do a second soak in acid to increase the chances of the dye striking the instant it touches the fiber. (If you are concerned about overacidifying your fibers, which can make them lose luster and strength, you can test your dye bath's pH with strips.)

Apply the dye with the method and tool of your choice. Even if you choose not to do an acid presoak, the acid in your dye mixture will be enough to fix the dye, but you can always give it a little boost by spritzing a bit of acid (either white vinegar or dissolved citric-acid crystals) onto your fibers with a spray bottle. Use the plastic wrap that is under your fiber to wrap it up burrito-style or carefully transfer it to new plastic. (Beware of excess dye or liquid running out the ends of the dye package and getting on your floor.)

Heat is required to set the dye, and some dyers use a microwave as a heat source. You can place the bundle of fiber in the microwave to heat, but you should use a separate microwave for dyeing than for food. Carefully check your dye package every 2 minutes—and I do mean carefully! Some microwaves heat unevenly, and one part of your dye parcel may be warm while the other side may be hot enough to create steam burns.

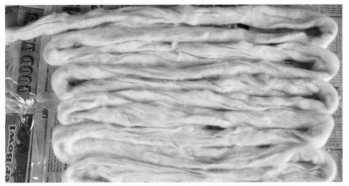

1. Cover your working surface with newspaper and plastic wrap, then lay out the fiber in manageable sections.

2. Dye can be applied with a syringe for fine control and small amounts.

4. I often use cut-up kitchen sponges to apply dye.

5. When you are satisfied with your dye application, roll up the fiber inside the plastic wrap like a burrito.

7. Place a colander or steamer in a slow cooker and add enough water to cover the bottom, but not so much that it seeps into the colander.

8. Place the entire burrito in the slow cooker and heat for 30 minutes or so.

3. A stencil brush can help apply dye through the fiber.

6. Make sure that the dye doesn't run out the ends of the burrito and stain other items.

9. Alternately, you can place the fiber directly on a baking sheet or oven-safe dish (such as the slow-cooker liner) and bake in the oven, spritzing with water to keep it moist.

If you prefer not to use a microwave, gently lift your fiber from the plastic wrap and quickly transfer it to a large baking sheet or another oven-safe item such as the porcelain insert from a slow cooker. Bake at 300°F (150°C) for 15 to 30 minutes, watching carefully. If the fiber appears to be drying out too quickly, spray it with water and cover loosely with foil or a lid if possible. You can also steam the fiber (in its plastic wrap) inside a slow cooker, using a colander or steamer to keep the fiber above the water level.

Once you have set the dye with heat, allow the fibers to return to room temperature. When dealing with colors that may not set well, are prone to bleeding, or don't exhaust completely (including some greens, reds, and blacks), try adding a small pinch of Synthrapol or washing soda to your rinse water to help shake loose any unset dye. Rinse and allow to dry using the same precautions as for kettle dyeing.

1. Lay out presoaked yarn the same as for handpainting fiber. To leave a white or undyed area, tie yarn or fabric around a section as a resist.

2. Apply the dye the same way as for handpainting fiber, being especially careful that the dye penetrates completely.

HANDPAINTING YARN Handpainting yarn is a very similar process to handpainting fiber. One exception is that the yarn will need to soak longer in warm water before you dye to ensure that all of the fibers are penetrated. The tighter the yarn is spun, the longer it will have to soak. To stop colors from running into one another or to create a section of white space, you can tie strips of cloth or yarn as a resist around the area where you want the dye to stop (such as for tie-dyeing). This technique could be used for fiber, but it's much more dramatic in yarn because the resist is more effective at keeping the colors from bleeding.

The biggest difference between handpainting fiber and yarn is that there is less room for error with yarn. When you make a mistake dyeing fibers, you can always pick out that section when you are preparing it for spinning. With yarn, you are pretty much committed to your happy accident, unless you overdye it or cut it out with scissors.

dyeing silk cocoons

Silk of all types looks spectacular when dyed; it can take on rich, bold hues. Silk cocoons can be especially fun to dye, and they add a wonderful pop of color to your yarn.

you will need:

* Silk cocoons
* Small container
* Water
* Prepared dye stock
* Slow cooker or other heat source and container
* Additional vinegar or other acidifier

Silk cocoons can be a bit tricky to dye because they float, leaving part of them exposed, and they need to be completely submerged for the dye to take evenly. I've found that they will take on sufficient water if you sink them with the handle of a spoon, staying down after becoming soaked.

Silk takes acid dye like wool does. (Silk is made of a different protein and unlike wool it can also be dyed with fiber-reactive dyes.) Dye takes to all kinds of silk quickly, so I don't add acid to the presoak. I refrain from using any acid in the dyebath until I am ready to heat it.

1. Silk cocoons can be dyed in a small container—even a glass of water.

2. Keep the cocoons submerged in the dyebath with the handles of spoons.

Dyeing Plant Fibers

The kind of dyes used for plant fibers are called fiber-reactive; they can be used for silk and some synthetic fibers as well as for cellulose.

Dyeing plant fibers is a bit different from dyeing wool, and it requires different preparation. In addition to fiber-reactive dye, you will need an activator such as soda ash as well as table salt.

you will need:

* Cellulose (plant-based) fiber or yarn (hemp, cotton, linen, etc.)

* Soda ash

* Water

* Sodium chloride (table salt)

* Fiber-reactive dye

When I first started dyeing plant fibers, all my results were pastels, no matter how much dye I used. A friend who does batik on cotton suggested adding the soda ash to my soaking bath instead of just the dyebath, which I've found helpful in achieving richer colors. Soak your fibers in water and soda ash for at least 30 minutes. Once you are confident they have been completely saturated, remove them and drain the excess water.

When the fiber is soaked, the instructions on the dye package will probably direct you to add dye to warm water, add fiber, wait, stir, and add salt and soda ash, being careful not to apply the soda ash directly onto the fiber. I've had better results by creating a mixture of warm water, dye, salt, and soda ash (following the proportions given on the dye instructions) and then stirring the elements until they're thoroughly combined before adding the fibers.

Unlike acid dyes, fiber-reactive dyes do not require heat to set, although the dyebath should be at least room temperature (about 75°F [24°C]). Some instructions suggest using water at 80° to 100°F (27° to 38°C), warm to hot tap temperature.

Although I have read that most of the dye is taken up by the fiber in the first half hour, I prefer to let these fiber-reactive dyes sit for at least an hour before draining and rinsing. Fiber-reactive dyes can react with water as well as fiber, so there will probably be a lot of color in your rinse water.

Find whatever dyeing method fits you like a glove—or better yet, make your own dyeing way. I find dyeing as gratifying as the spinning of yarn and knitting of garments. It also allows you complete control over your artistic process.

dyed hemp top

1. Add soda ash to your soaking bath for richer colors.

2. Allow the fibers to soak for at least 30 minutes.

3. While the fibers are soaking, add dye to warm water.

4. Add salt and soda ash to the dyebath.

5. Add the fiber to the dyebath and allow it to sit for an hour or more.

blend fiber & color

Look at your fibers themselves as a part of a palette. This approach to the materials of your yarn is part of what makes it art yarn and not simply novelty yarn. You can use a drumcarder to create blends of a wide variety of fibers, colors, and textures, making batts that are completely unique to your vision—restrained, over the top, or somewhere in between.

Using a Drumcarder

A drumcarder is a wonderful tool that can completely transform your spinning. It's also a specialized and expensive piece of equipment that requires practice to use well. (If you'd like to practice before investing in a drumcarder, inquire with your local spinning guild; many have carders that can be rented by guild members.)

parts of the drumcarder

There are several major components to any drumcarder: the tray that holds the fiber ready to be carded; the licker-in, or small roller in the front, which pulls the fiber in; the main drum, which is the larger piece where the batt will build up; and the drive band or chain. Depending on whether the carder is manual or electric, it will have either a hand crank or a motor to turn the licker-in and large drum. Drumcarders should also come with a doffer, a tool that looks like a long ice pick, which is used to remove the batt from the drum, and clamps to hold the carder in place on the table.

licker-in

drive band

main drum

hand crank

clamps

Although drumcarders are fairly safe, the teeth in the carding cloth are very sharp and the piece is heavy. Keep your fingers clear of the drums, especially when they are turning, and secure the carder so that it doesn't slide or fall.

adding fiber

To add fiber to the carder, lay it in the tray so that it touches the licker-in, then keep your hands clear and allow the licker-in to pull the fiber onto the drum. (There is no need to push it; the fiber will be drawn in on its own.) Add fiber to the carder in small batches; the batt will build up on the drum in layers, not all at once.

When you have added all the fiber you want to or the drum is full, stop turning it and remove the batt. You will know that the drum is full when the fiber nearly reaches the top of the teeth. Find the seam or strip on the main drum where there are no teeth and slide the doffer beneath the layer of fibers there. Pull the tool up gently until the batt pulls away from the drum and opens there; you may need to do this in several steps. Gently peel the batt off the carder, grasping the fibers firmly.

It may be necessary to run a batt through the carder several times to fully blend it. For additional passes through the carder, strip the original batt by pulling a piece off the side. Place each piece in the tray individually and allow it to be transferred to the main drum before adding the next strip.

Over time, pieces of fiber will become caught in the teeth of the licker-in and main drum, and fine lint will accumulate around the moving parts and under the carder. Periodically clean the carder by gently brushing off any fiber from the drum, then use tweezers if necessary to remove fiber and lint.

USING A DRUMCARDER

1. Place the fiber to be carded in the tray little by little and keep your hands clear as you card.

2. When the fiber builds up to the height of the teeth on the main drum, it's full.

3. When the drum is full, insert the tool beneath the fiber along the seam of the main drum.

4. Raise the tool to divide the batt for removal.

5. Use the tool to separate the batt at the seam. (It may be necessary to do it one section at a time.)

6. Grasp the fibers and gently pull the batt off the back of the carder.

An Exercise in Blending Fibers

Use a drumcarder to create unique combinations and textures that express a variety of ideas in your yarn. A drumcarder can blend all different kinds of fiber—natural and synthetic, long and short, plant and animal. Making this thoroughly blended batt will teach you a range of carding skills and produce a rich material for yarn.

you will need:

* A drumcarder, including the tools to clamp it to the table and remove the batt
* A few ounces of the fibers you'd like to blend (here, alpaca, bison, hemp, nylon glitz, sari silk, silk noil, wool)

Mixing a short, soft fiber such as angora with a long, initially stiff fiber such as hemp can create a nicely balanced batt if blended well. If they are not blended enough, the shorter fibers will not be incorporated equally with the longer fibers. Taken as single parts, they may not create the "ideal" yarn, but blended together they create a rich symphony.

When you spin your blend, you might find those shorter fibers clumped together, separating more from the longer ones. (In some instances that may be an attractive and desirable characteristic; it primarily depends on the yarn you intend to create.) Blending different fibers can be tricky, because very short or fine fibers such as angora do not react well to multiple trips through the drumcarder. Finding the right balance of blending thoroughly without damaging the fibers comes only with practice.

A blended batt (center) and its components

batt recipe

Combine a wide variety of fibers to create this rich and unique blended batt. Start with equal parts (1½ ounces [43 g]) alpaca, Navajo churro, hemp, and bison, plus about ¼ ounce (7 g) each of silk noil, recycled sari silk, and glitz (nylon). Each fiber contributes a special quality to the finished product: the alpaca and bison will add softness, the Navajo churro will add body, the silk noil will add texture, and the hemp will add both texture and strength. The recycled silk sari will add color that will not be diluted when blended with other fibers, and the glitz will add sparkle. (Before you run the sari silk through the carder, cut it up into "bite-sized" 2-inch [5 cm] bits. Otherwise, it can wrap around the drum of your carder and cause havoc.)

begin to blend

Begin by blending the alpaca and churro into their own individual batts, then combine the bison, silk noil, hemp, nylon glitz, and recycled sari silk into a separate batt. Once these three batts are assembled, remove a strip from each and run them through the carder in alternating layers. (When the large drum is full, stop adding fiber, remove the batt, and start a new batt. You may need to make several batts to use all of the fiber.) After the first pass through the carder you should have something that looks like a sandwich. For thorough blending, rip off small strips from this new batt and pass them through the carder; it can take three or more passes to get a good distribution of fibers.

1. Card the alpaca and Navajo churro into separate batts.

2. Card the bison, hemp, silk noil, and glitz into one batt.

3. Add the recycled sari silk to the bison, hemp, noil, and glitz batt.

4. Tear a strip from each of the three batts and card it again, passing the strip back and forth in the tray to apply it to the full width of the drum.

5. After the first pass, the batt will have distinct layers.

6. After being stripped and carded several times, the batt will be thoroughly integrated.

An Exercise in Color

Blending colors with a drumcarder can be as simple or complex as you make it, from a single-color batt to a deliberately striped one. Just as a painter blends colors to create the precise hue needed, you can blend different colors of fiber to create lighter, darker, or more complex shades from basic solids. Carding can be especially effective to make one popular type of yarn that gradually shifts color, making long stripes or sections of color when worked up. To create such a yarn, start with a few solid colors plus black and white.

you will need:

* A drumcarder, including the tools to clamp it to the table and remove the batt
* 1½ ounces (43 g) each of green, blue, and purple top or roving, along with ¼ ounce (7 g) each of black and white

begin to blend

Card the three colors of top individually to create a solid-color batt from each; run them through the carder at least two times so all the fibers are equally blended. The more they go through the drumcarder, the more even your finished batts will be, but keep in mind that shorter fibers such as merino tend to nep the more they are carded.

Start the color blending with green. Using a scale to measure accurately, add ¼ ounce (7 g) of white to ½ ounce (14 g) of green. Alternating layers, card strips of green and white into one batt. After the first pass, the batt will have layers of green and white; strip the batt and blend it a second (and possibly a third) time until the batt is an even light green.

Next, make the green-to-blue and blue-to-purple mixtures: Blend ½ ounce each of the green and blue batts in the same way as for the green and white and blend ½ ounce (14 g) each of blue and purple together. Blend ½ ounce (14 g) of the purple with ¼ ounce (7 g) of black as for the white and green to create a darker purple.

By blending these three main colors on the carder in different combinations, you create four colors that will change gently as the yarn is spun. This blended set can be spun any way you like it. Make long sections of color by spinning each batt in order until all of the fiber is used up, or divide each section of color into smaller pieces and alternate them in order for shorter sections.

BLENDING SHADED COLORS

1. Card 1½ ounces (43 g) each of green, blue, and purple separately.

2. Measure ½ ounce (14 g) of green and ¼ ounce (7 g) of white.

3. Add strips of green and white alternately to blend the batts together.

4. After the first pass, the batt has distinct layers.

5. Strip the layered batt and card it again to make a solid light green batt.

6. Repeat the process of stripping and carding until the colors are fully blended, then repeat for the other colors.

shades of color series

By measuring and blending batts from three original colors plus black and white, you can create four additional colors for a gentle transition around the color wheel.

$^{1}/_{4}$ ounce
(7 g)

$^{1}/_{2}$ ounce
(14 g)

$^{1}/_{2}$ ounce
(14 g)

$^{1}/_{2}$ ounce
(14 g)

$^1/_2$ ounce
(14 g)

$^1/_2$ ounce
(14 g)

$^1/_2$ ounce
(14 g)

$^1/_4$ ounce
(7 g)

spinning basics

Spinning consistently before making art yarn is akin to learning to crawl before you can run. Sometimes happy accidents do occur, but the problem with a happy accident is that more often than not, you can't re-create them—so the technique is lost and nothing is learned. A successful art yarn can survive its intended use, and a successful spinner must be able to use basic techniques to create any yarn at will.

Predrafting

There are many reasons why preparation is important. The more you prepare your fiber, the better your yarn will be. Although some types of yarn may be better spun without predrafting, spinning art yarn is one case in which extra preparation before spinning can be especially helpful.

The more thoughtful predrafting you do, the more you can concentrate on spinning and focus on getting your yarn just the way you want. When spinning an art yarn, your hands are often occupied with three (or more) simultaneous tasks: introducing new fiber into the twist, regulating the twist, and keeping some fibers out of the twist. Predrafting lets you take care of some of these before you sit down so that you can concentrate on others. Predrafting can also be useful if you plan to make a deliberately uneven yarn; while spinning, your hands tend to move in a consistent rhythm, which can make it difficult to get varied effects in the same yarn.

Whether you are using combed top, roving, or batts, the act of predrafting is nearly the same. There are two major methods of predrafting: stripping and stretching. The fiber source may be too wide for you to handle easily, especially when working with a batt, so you will probably want to divide the fiber source lengthwise. The fiber should be predrafted to correspond to the size of your desired yarn, but not thinner. When making a thin yarn, my predrafted strips are about a quarter of the size of a pencil. While you are stripping the fiber, keep an eye out for neps, noils, and other undesirable bits of fiber. Pick them out now so you won't have to stop while spinning.

After you separate the fiber into thinner strips, it can be helpful to pull the fibers apart, especially with compacted commercially prepared top. (This is sometimes referred to as "cracking the whip.") Firmly grip one end of the fiber with one hand, placing your other hand several inches down the length. Gently tug so that the individual fibers separate slightly from their neighbors. You should be able to feel when you have tugged enough because your hands meet with less resistance. Move down the length of fiber and repeat until all the fibers have been drawn out (or attenuated). This final step makes the fibers glide into the drafting triangle almost effortlessly, leaving your fingers free to control the twist.

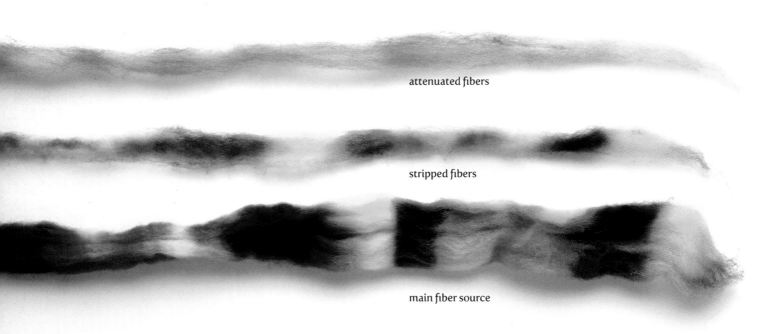

attenuated fibers

stripped fibers

main fiber source

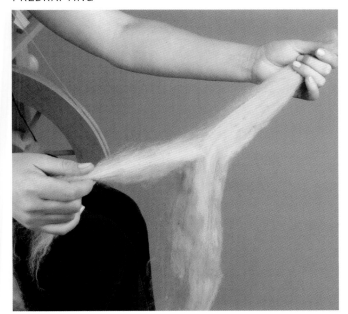 

1. To prepare a carded batt for spinning, grasp a piece at the edge of one end and pull it down and to the side. Continue to pull the piece apart along the "grain" of the batt.

2. Holding combed top at the end, pull a strip off the side.

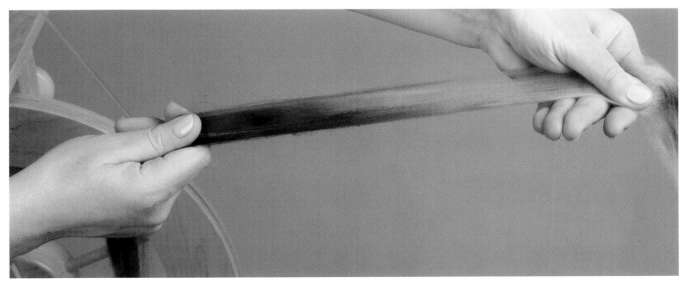

3. Gently pull the fiber supply lengthwise so that the fibers are loosened but don't separate completely.

Fundamental Singles

Before you can create well-made art yarns, you need to master a few basic spinning techniques. These yarns are like white sauce in a chef's repertoire: the solid basis for exciting experimentation and innovation.

high-twist singles

You may be thinking, "High-twist singles are not art yarn." By themselves, perhaps not (though art is in the eye of the beholder). But spinning stable singles is an important technique for creating yarns that are structurally sound.

you will need:

* Fiber (batt, top or roving), predrafted to spin smoothly and easily

High-twist singles are essential components of classic yarns, but they are also major components in art yarns. I use them to secure other elements, ply with thicker yarns, string add-ins, and a million other things. We want a functional, well-constructed art yarn that will stand the test of time, not be a waste of the spinner's time.

Most of the fine singles in my spinning come from batts. I like to spin fine singles from blends of fibers such as nylon glitz and recycled sari silk; to me, these fibers look better spun fine. These singles can add subtle details to a finished yarn, little touches of color or flashes of light that complete the yarn. The subtle color play can pull everything together, creating a holistic yarn.

To spin a high-twist yarn, you will need to draft somewhat quickly and add a lot of twist to keep it together. Choose a smaller whorl to add twist quickly; if your wheel isn't equipped with a range of whorls, you will find yourself treadling very quickly. Attach the fiber to your leader and treadle at a comfortable pace, drafting out fiber regularly to produce an even yarn. If possible, set the tension or brake fairly low so that the yarn isn't pulled away from you, which could make the yarn break or keep you from making the yarn fine enough.

For a smoother, more worsted-style yarn, pull the fiber forward toward the orifice and smooth the twist back to your fiber hand. For a loftier, more woolen-style yarn, let the twist grab some of the fiber and pull back against it gently. (The second method may take more practice, and the yarn may not be quite as even.)

To see whether the yarn has enough twist to hold up, pull out a length and let it twist back on itself. You can decide by looking at it or by comparing it with the measurement tables on page 61 whether the singles you're spinning will be suitable for your end use.

FINE HIGH-TWIST SINGLES

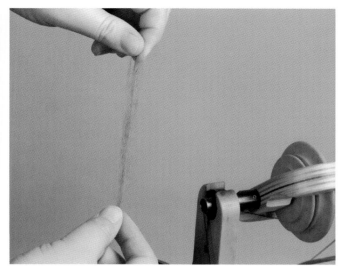

1. Predraft the fiber thoroughly for fine yarn.

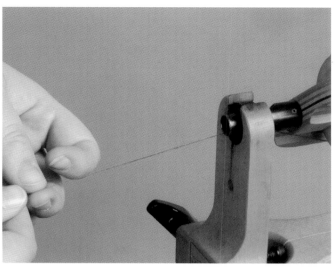

2. For a smooth worsted-style yarn, draft the fibers forward and smooth them back.

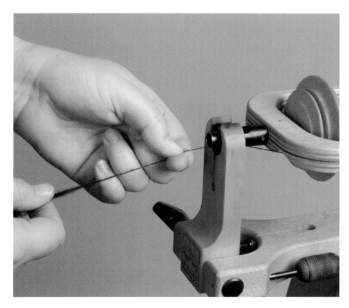

3. For a woolen-style yarn, let twist run behind your front hand.

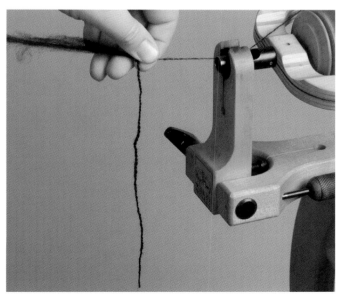

4. Allow a length of yarn to twist back on itself to determine whether the yarn has enough twist.

bulky singles

Almost all spinners find that after the initial learning curve it is much easier to spin thin yarns than thick ones. Thick, fluffy singles can add lots of color and soft texture to an art yarn, so they're worth the practice.

you will need:

* Fiber (batt, top or roving), predrafted to spin smoothly and easily

To make bulky singles, predraft the fiber carefully. Especially if I haven't spun fat yarn in a while, I may predraft the fiber almost down to the size of the finished yarn I want. When your hands are more comfortable with the technique, you may be able to predraft less. You can make this yarn with batts, roving, or top, but I prefer the sleeker look of top in bulky singles.

To spin thick yarn, choose a larger whorl and use more tension than for thin yarn. Attach the yarn to your leader and try not to treadle too fast as you draft. The more twist you add, the thinner the yarn will want to be; fat yarn holds a lot less twist. Periodically stop and make sure that you haven't unconsciously started spinning finer yarn as you fall into a rhythm.

A good way to judge is to measure and weigh your finished yarn. Bulky yarn should weigh around 600 to 800 yards (546 to 728 m) per pound (454 g). If your yarn weighs significantly more but still measures about 10 wpi, you may want to revisit how you are predrafting. You can also try just treadling slowly—even painfully slowly!—without any fiber as an exercise in maintaining a slow, steady rhythm. (This can be a helpful exercise for any spinner, spinning for any type of yarn.)

BULKY SINGLES

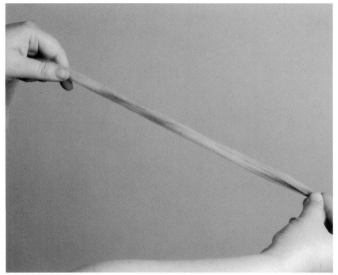

1. Predraft the fiber almost to the size of the finished yarn.

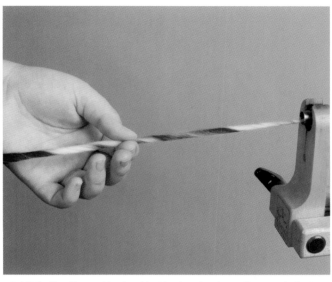

2. With the fiber attached to the leader, treadle evenly but not too fast.

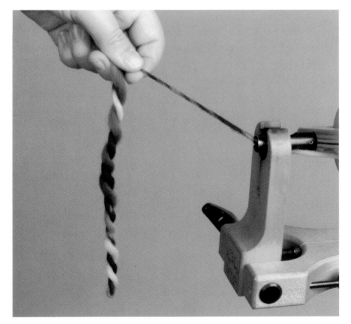

3. Bulky yarn requires a lot less twist to hold together, and it can create vivid areas of bright color.

thick-and-thin singles

Most of us start out spinning slubby yarn, then start to make finer and more evenly spun yarns once we tune our drafting skills and gain more control. It can be difficult to return to spinning that slubby stuff that was so easy at the beginning. This yarn has sections of higher twist (which corresponds with thinner yarn) and lower twist (thicker yarn). It's an excellent way to practice sensing and controlling twist.

you will need:

* Fiber (batts, top, or roving), predrafted as needed

Spinning a slubby yarn requires different control and rhythm than spinning a smooth, fine yarn and entails synchronizing the body (hands and feet) with the senses (sight and touch). Spinning slubby and bulky yarns is ideal to cut your art yarn teeth on—there isn't much juggling of fibers and feet, so it can be a great confidence booster.

The first step in spinning thick-and-thin is the same as for every yarn: fiber selection and preparation. Use a combed top for two reasons: the shorter and weaker fibers are eliminated, and the parallel alignment of the fibers helps create slubs. The more you predraft, the less you will need to draft while spinning, giving you more opportunity to concentrate on the twist entering your yarn. When you are attenuating the fibers, allow some unevenness; thicker and thinner portions of fiber supply will help create variety in the yarn.

SPINNING SLUBS Start by spinning up to a yard of worsted-weight yarn, drafting the fiber evenly, to ensure that your fibers are connected to your leader and to establish your natural rhythm. Soon you will come to an area where your predrafting and the staple length of the fibers have created good conditions for a slub. To spin a slub, relax your twist-control pinching hand and steadily slow the treadling speed. Allow the twist to glide over the slub. (A bulky yarn requires far fewer twists per inch to hold together, as little as one twist per inch.)

The length of the fiber and your natural drafting rhythm will dictate the frequency of the slubs. Your arms and hands will develop a particular distance that they draft out the fibers, and eventually they will draft almost exactly the same distance each time.

SPINNING THIN Part of the drama of a slubby yarn is adding thin parts between the thick parts for contrast. As with any yarn, predrafting dictates the size of the yarn, and drafting finer will produce a thinner section of yarn. When you were attenuating the fibers (the second step of predrafting), the midpoint of the fiber between your hands probably created a thinner section where one fiber's staple ended and another began.

Just as you slowed your treadling for the bulky slub, speed up the treadling to create a stable fine section. Practice finding the balance between overspinning the slubs (treadling too fast) and adding enough twist to the finer sections.

SPINNING SLUBS

1. Start spinning a length of worsted-weight yarn.

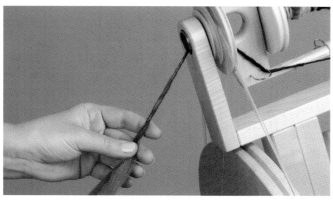

2. Relax your twist-control hand while slowing your treadling.

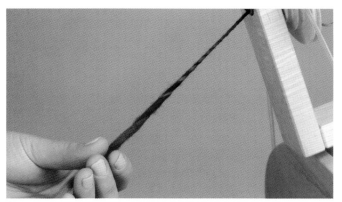

3. The twist will glide over the slub, holding it together.

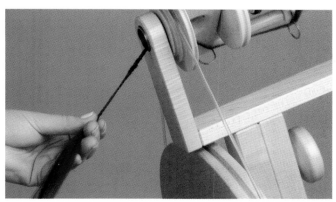

4. When you come to a thin spot in the fiber, speed up your treadling.

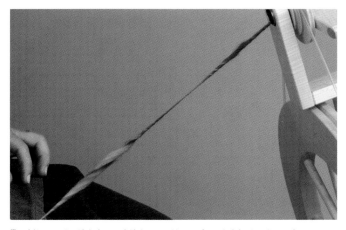

5. Alternate thick and thin portions for richly textured yarn.

Handspun versus Millspun

It may sound appealing to use a millspun yarn instead of creating a thin consistent yarn. Using thread has advantages but also some serious drawbacks. First, commercial yarn probably won't evolve with your yarn through washing, knitting, or wearing. If you are stringing silk cocoons (see page 94), sewing thread won't grip the way wool singles (with their natural follicles) will. With wear, the sewing thread will work its way out of the yarn, leaving you with a cocoon on a string. Commercial binders have often been tamed in the manufacturing process, removing the fiber's character. Handspun yarn is full of energy and life.

Second, creating yarns out of handspun components makes them that much more inventive and special—more time-consuming, but ultimately more gratifying and satisfying. If you are going through the trouble to make a beaded yarn, the step of spinning suitable singles isn't that much more work in the grand scheme of things.

There are exceptions, especially when a thread or commercial binder is not a major component in your yarn. Sometimes the integrity of the yarn does not hinge on the commercial thread, such as when wrapping filament up and down the length of a single; the filament is merely a nonessential decoration. A thread may have properties such as glowing in the dark or elasticity that aren't feasible with handspun yarn. I also make an exception when spinning coils; nothing beats fine crochet cotton for drape and hand, providing a highly workable hank of coils. Coils made with a handspun core are stiffer and more difficult to knit with, but they don't come uncoiled as easily when the yarn is cut.

Weights and Measures

Knowing how to measure your yarn by various means is a useful skill, particularly when you want to work a pattern written for commercial yarn in your own yarn creations. There are numerous charts of measurements and formulas. What most don't explain, however, is that you really have to know your own yarn and your own spinning techniques to measure them accurately.

wraps per inch

The easiest yarn measurement to find is the wraps per inch (wpi). Simply wrap the yarn around a ruler for an inch or more, count the number of strands, and divide if necessary to find the wpi. (Be careful not to stretch the yarn or squish it too tight while measuring, which will make the yarn seem thinner than it really is.) Yarn with high wraps per inch is thinner; yarn with low wraps per inch is thicker.

This measurement is closely linked with the needle size or weaving sett; yarns with fewer wraps per inch have a fatter diameter, which means a larger needle size or a looser sett. For a yarn such as slubby singles or beaded yarn, you may not be able to measure the wraps per inch accurately with a small sample. The number of wraps per inch will likely go down during finishing if the yarn blooms.

yards per pound

Yards per pound (ypp) is the other most common measurement of a yarn. The simplest way to find the yards per pound is to measure the yardage, then weigh the skein. You'll need to do some simple math—divide the number of ounces in the skein by 16 (the number of ounces in a pound), then divide the number of yards in the skein by that fraction. (A 200-yard skein that weighs 2 ounces has 1,600 yards per pound.)

The yards per pound helps you find the density of a skein of yarn. For example, if two yarns have 12 wraps per inch but one has 1,200 yards per pound and the other only 800, the second yarn is a lot denser than the first. It may be stiff and not lofty. The yardage per pound also depends on the fiber and drafting method; a softly spun yarn has more yards per pound than a smooth worsted yarn, and silk yarn has more yards per pound than wool, even at the same number of wraps per inch. (Needless to say, art yarns may break the mold here, too—yarns with glass beads weigh more than yarns without them.)

The weight and length of a skein can give you the yards per pound.

Measure wraps per inch with a ruler.

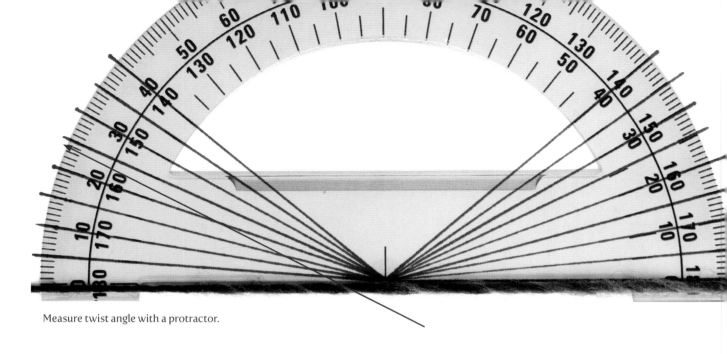

Measure twist angle with a protractor.

twist angle

Twist angle is a bit trickier to measure, but it can give you some really useful information. Measuring twist angle is easier than it sounds. You'll need a protractor, a pen, and a sheet of paper. Start by drawing a line down the center of the paper, which will serve as your baseline. Line up the bottom of the protractor with the straight line and mark the center of the protractor and angles along the edge in 5° increments. Draw straight lines from the starting point to each 5° increment. Place your yarn along the straight line and look for the angle line that best matches the angle of twist in your yarn. It may be easier to see if you lay a needle along the twist. It's easier to see the angle of twist in plied yarn or singles with color variations.

The twist angle tells you how tightly a yarn is spun. Yarn with a twist angle of 10° is much more softly spun than yarn with a twist angle of 35°. Yarns made from short fibers need more twist to hold together than yarns made from longer fibers, so a cotton yarn would probably have a higher twist angle than a silk yarn.

twists per inch

While the yarn is stretched out to measure twist angle, you may be able to see the twists per inch (tpi) most clearly. Hold your yarn next to a ruler and see how many times the twist runs through the yarn in one inch. You may find it easiest to observe this on a yarn with clear definition between light and dark.

Like twist angle, the number of twists per inch is a measure of how much twist is in a yarn. Bulky yarns have fewer twists per inch; fine yarns have more. In a thick-and-thin yarn, the twist angle should stay relatively constant throughout for the yarn to be structurally sound, but as the thickness of the yarn changes, the number of twists per inch changes, too. Although they're related, the two measurements give you different pictures of the yarn.

Measure twists per inch with a ruler.

making sense of measurements

These techniques may seem out of place in art yarn. No number alone is the definitive way to measure yarn. It's clear that we can't figure out a yarn's "weight" by weighing alone. Using wpi and ypp doesn't account for the inconsistencies that naturally occur with handspinning, and it would be insufficient for a coiled or core-spun yarn.

So why is it important to know these things? These measuring techniques can be useful in troubleshooting. For instance, if you have a yarn spun from locks that pulls apart when you use it, consider the story that the numbers tell. The weight (in ypp) may be spot-on for the number of wraps per inch because uncarded fibers tend to draft more densely and parts of the locks are not incorporated into the twist. Look at the number of twists per inch and the twist angle to see whether the twist is sufficient. One of my very first yarns measured about 10 wraps per inch but weighed well over a pound for 500 yards and had about 3 tpi. In other words, for its diameter the yarn was very heavy and was overspun in places. The yarn had no loft because I hadn't learned proper drafting.

A helpful exercise to see where your yarn falls on the spectrum is to spin a single without fancy add-ins or embellishments in the same fibers you intend to use in your art yarn. Measure it to see the properties of the fiber and then compare it with a yarn using more unconventional techniques. Knowing the rules and how to spin within them will help create an art yarn that is not only useful but also structurally sound.

As your spinning evolves, the weight of your yarn will decrease at least a small amount (meaning more yards per pound) as your drafting ability gets better. Your tpi will naturally follow suit—as the number of yards per pound and the wraps per inch increase, the number of twists per inch does, too.

Some Approximations for Plain Yarns

Yarn weight	Yards per pound (ypp)	Wraps per inch (wpi)
lace	2,600+	18+
fingering	1,900–2,400	16
sport	1,200–1,800	14
worsted	900–1,200	12
bulky	600–800	10
very bulky	400–500	8 or fewer

Angle of Twist
The angle of twist depends on the individual yarn, with a higher number indicating more twist.

Twists per Inch
The number of twists per inch depends on the individual yarn. With other factors held constant, yarns with more yards per pound have more twists per inch.

Finishing Yarn

The last step in your art yarns can be among the most important: setting the twist and finishing. Most yarns share basic techniques for finishing, though some require special treatment.

Set the twist of most yarns with a soapy hot-water wash, a dunk in cold water, and a clean (soapless) hot bath. The dunk in cold water "shocks" the fibers, especially wool, and helps them adhere to each other a little. This makes the yarn more cohesive and stable, as the follicles of different elements grab onto each other. After rinsing, wring it out and give it a good whack on the floor or the side of the tub or sink. This will help the fibers bloom.

For yarns with added elements made from fiber blends, think about the yarn's composition to decide about finishing. Sari silk tends to bleed a lot in the wash, so add plenty of vinegar to the rinse. For blended yarns, I use the finishing method for the majority fiber, which is usually wool. For yarns with fragile elements, you might want to omit the thwack.

The basics may sound boring when you're eager to start creating, but understanding the hows and whys of all kinds of yarn will help you make yarns that look as great after years of use as when you first dream them up. These are skills you'll return to again and again as your spinning abilities grow.

1. Immerse the yarn in hot, soapy water to set the twist.

2. Follow the hot, soapy bath with a cold dunk and a final rinse in hot clean water. Wring out the yarn, give it a good thwack, and allow it to dry.

uncarded fiber

Whether they're combined with prepared fiber or making up a yarn by themselves, uncarded locks can add a wild yet luxurious dimension to art yarn. Spinning uncarded fibers highlights the natural crimp of the fibers. Using vivid color combinations together with more natural shades creates a striking effect. Locks can be added as an accent or can be the structural element of a yarn. It can be as simple as grabbing clumps of wool and adding them into the twist or more thoroughly thought out, using specific color schemes and manipulating the individual fibers precisely.

Spinning Uncarded Locks

Instead of combing or carding washed wool, you can spin it just as it is, making a yarn that is colorful and richly textured. This technique is easier with long locks that can build up some twist before it's time to add another.

you will need:

* Clean, washed locks; dyed mohair or longwool is preferable

It can be helpful to start with a large bunch of fibers and draft them out, tugging the fibers gently with both hands. After washing and dyeing, uncarded fibers can clump, so loosen them up. Using a smaller piece helps the fibers grip your leader, ensuring a secure start to your yarn. Add in locks from the cut end (see Lock Structure, below right), teasing them out slightly with your fingers to help them grip the fibers already in the twist.

After you have the first lock attached to your leader, pretty much anything goes—add in longer bits, shorter bits, or flyaway locks. When the twist has firmly secured one lock, repeat the process to add more. The joins will probably not be smooth, and the finished yarn will be lumpy, bumpy, and curly.

I find it necessary to juggle at least two separate sets of fiber while at the same time regulating the twist. This is especially true when the fibers are of substantially different lengths. You may find it helpful to alternate which lock is acting as a "core" while the other wraps around. This ensures that enough of the fibers are trapped in and makes an interesting texture as well.

Lock Structure

To add unprocessed fiber successfully, you need to understand the structure of locks. Like our hair, wool and similar fibers have scales that feel smooth in one direction (from cut end to tip) and rough in the other (from tip to cut end). If left outside the twist to float free, the cut ends will felt. Add the cut ends first to make sure they are not outside the twist. Otherwise, they will eventually start to look worn. Even in this free-spirited yarn, the lock end should remain curly and crimpy even with wear.

SPINNING UNCARDED FIBER

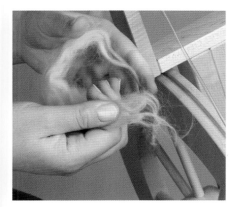

1. Begin with a clump of locks larger than you could comfortably draft.

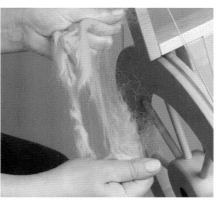

2. Tug the fibers apart to open them up so that the twist can grab them.

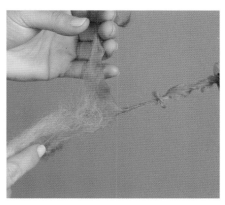

3. Tease out the cut ends so that the twist can grasp them firmly.

4. Both hands will be busy holding the fiber and managing the twist. Alternate which hand holds a lock to the side.

5. Holding one lock to the side allows it to wrap around the core, blending the colors and also securing the joins.

6. When one or two locks are firmly anchored in the twist, you can start another.

7. Using different colors and lengths of locks creates a vibrant palette and texture.

Spinning Prepared and Unprepared Fibers

You can alternate using combed or carded wool with locks to make the untamed fibers really "pop." Prepared fibers are generally easier to work with than locks are; depending on the preparation method, the fibers are all loosened or going in the same direction. Using unprepared fibers will create more texture and provide a unique look to the yarn.

you will need:

* Prepared fiber (batts, roving, or top)
* Clean wool locks

To secure a lock in a yarn made from prepared fibers, separate the fiber already in the drafting triangle and place the cut ends of the locks in the center. (You may need to stop treadling or untwist the yarn slightly to open the drafting triangle.) Firmly pinch the point of twist with your fingers and resume normal treadling speed, gradually loosening your pinch on the drafting zone and allowing the twist to engulf the new fibers. This is especially effective if you are core spinning the new addition (see page 76), which is an easy way to put the cut ends in the twist, because everything that needs to find its way into the twist is present.

ADDING LOCKS TO PREPARED FIBER

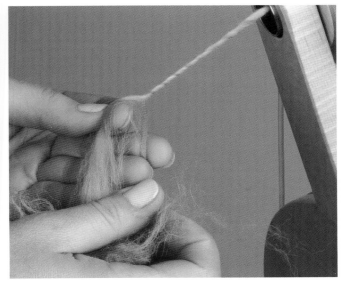

1. Divide the fiber in the drafting triangle and add the new fiber (cut ends first) between the halves.

2. Pinch the fibers at the point of twist.

3. After building up more twist by treadling, allow the twist into the fibers.

Free-flowing Locks

Who can resist the look of roaming locks? Not me! I love the soft, wavy look of yarns in which the locks are free to curl and stand out from the yarn. Although the previous two techniques taught you to add locks as a building block of yarns, this one will allow you to add locks that are firmly attached yet free to float above the surface. This is a great way to use very fine, soft locks, such as kid mohair or Lincoln wool.

you will need:

* Clean high-quality locks of mohair or longwool
* Top, roving, or batts (optional)

One way to create a free-flowing lock is simply to hold the tip end of a section of locks out of the twist. Identify which locks you would like to stand out and isolate them just before they reach the drafting triangle. Keep one end within the twist enough to make the yarn structurally sound, but keep the rest of the lock out of the twist. The volume of the undrafted fibers will allow the twist to skim over the lock. (Remember that the thicker the yarn, the less twist it holds, so the twist won't accumulate as much in the bulkier section.)

Another way to achieve a free-flowing-lock look is to keep locks out of the twist by almost plucking them out. Treadling slowly, take the locks in your hands and gently tease out the cut ends (the parts that will felt). Lay the locks over the core. (The core shown here is combed top, but you could spin it from batts, unprocessed fibers, a combed top, handspun singles, fabric—anything that can hold twist.) Release the lock slowly, allowing the ends to be engulfed by the twist. Then hold the section you wish to leave loose free from the twist. Enough of the ends should be trapped in the yarn to keep the lock secure while giving the appearance of floating above the yarn. To make sure that the locks are firmly included, give them a gentle tug after spinning a few more inches. If you are able to pull any out, you can try to add them again.

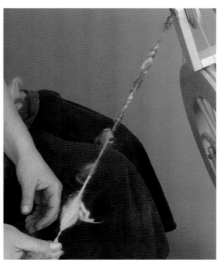

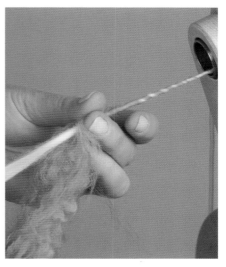

1. To skim the twist over a lock, isolate the lock that you want to leave free.

2. The twist will run through the lock but leave most of the fibers loose.

3. To pluck a lock out to float free, hold the lock over the core while treadling slowly.

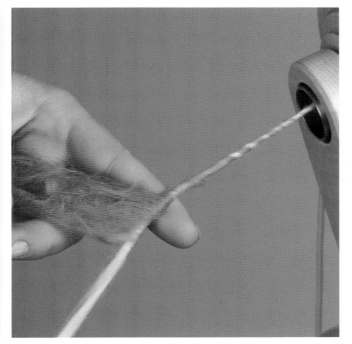

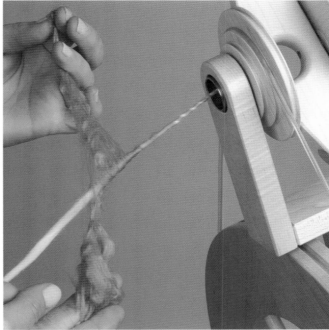

4. Hold the fibers you want uncaptured away from the twist.

5. Release the fibers gradually, allowing the ends to be caught in the twist.

core spinning

Core spinning is the single most useful technique in creating art yarns. In one way or another, the basic principles of core spinning always seem to come up, especially when spinning fabrics, using wool locks, and making textural wool "chrysalides" on singles. It's especially useful when spinning items that may not draft like traditional spinning fibers. It also helps to encase and secure the beginnings and ends (and sometimes middles!) of elements that may not have been entirely caught in the drafting triangle. The act of core spinning is simple, and once you have a good grasp on this tool, you can employ it in many different situations.

Thread, crochet cotton, a single, a ribbon—anything can act as your "core." Core spinning consists of adding fiber on a core and allowing fiber to find the twist and be laid over the core.

Core spinning captures fibers in the twist that is being added to the core; as the twist accumulates, it can pick up and incorporate other fibers along with the base. To keep the core and the final yarn stable, you will most often spin in the direction that the core was last twisted; check for the direction of twist, if there is one. (Elastic threads, nylon serger thread, and other cores may be extruded with no twist added; you can twist them in either direction.) Because you are adding twist to a yarn that was previously stable, the resulting core-spun yarn will be energized to some degree. You can decide whether to ply it to be more balanced or use it in its energized state.

blended batt core-spun
with elastic thread

Elastic Core

To explore the most basic application of this technique, we'll add fiber to a commercial thread. To spice things up a bit, we will use an elastic thread. I have chosen a batt to demonstrate; for the fine application of fiber over the elastic core, I find this preparation easier to core spin than top.

you will need

* Elastic thread
* Fiber as desired

Use an overhand knot to tie the elastic directly to the leader yarn. Tear off a small strip of the batt and hold it in your left hand. Treadling and holding the elastic taut with your right hand, allow individual fibers to find and be caught by the twist; you will feel them pulled out of your hand. The twist is what takes the fiber from your hand; you aren't drafting it so much as introducing it to the twist building up in the core, and then the magic happens. As long as the core thread remains taut, the twist is doing all of the work for you.

As more fibers find the twist, you can regulate how the fiber is laid over the elastic core. More fibers laid over the core create a thicker yarn; less fiber, a thinner yarn. As you continue "feeding" fiber to the accumulating twist in the core, decide how much fiber to add and what angle to hold it at.

SPINNING ON AN ELASTIC CORE

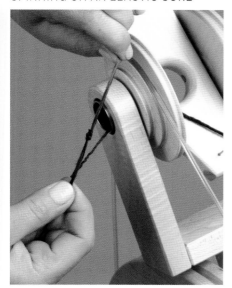

1. Tie the core to the leader yarn with an overhand knot.

2. Tear off a strip of batt.

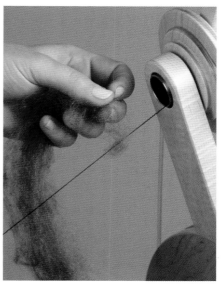

3. Hold the fiber over the elastic core as you begin adding twist.

4. As the twist enters the core, it traps fiber.

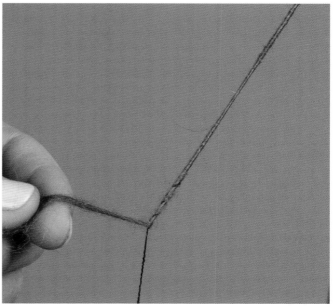

5. The outer fiber covers the core completely, hiding the base as much as you like.

Core-spun Locks

To add texture and color to your core-spun yarn, you can add in a different type of fiber, such as locks.

Tease out the cut ends of the fiber to give the twist plenty of surface to grab (see page 66). Just as you did for the batt, hold the lock in your left hand with the cut end over the core, allowing individual fibers to find the twist. To make the locks stand out and keep them concentrated in one area, manipulate each lock by holding it perpendicular to the core so that it wraps around it completely. Pinch the twist firmly to keep more twist from going in and to push the fibers more thoroughly into the core and add more fiber, either from a batt or from another lock.

you will need

* Clean dyed or undyed locks of fiber; mohair or longwool are good choices

* Fiber (batts, roving, or top, predrafted; optional)

* Thread, prespun yarn, or elastic (core)

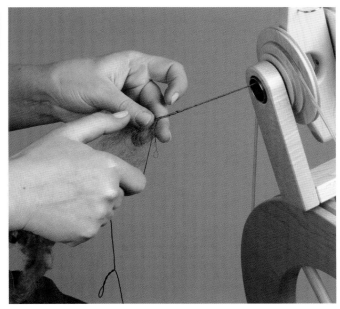

1. Fluff out the cut end of the lock and hold it where the twist can grab it.

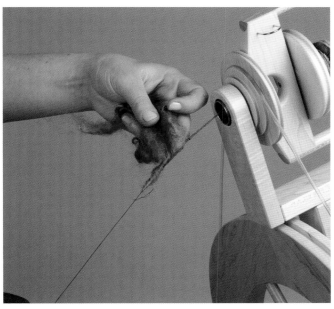

2. When the end of the lock has been anchored in the twist, hold it out at a 90° angle so it can wrap around the core fully.

3. When the lock has been fully incorporated, pinch the twist firmly and hold additional fiber against the core.

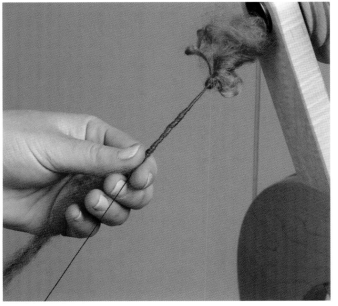

4. Mix locks, batts, and other fibers as desired.

Wool Chrysalis

Another yarn that uses core-spinning techniques is the "wool chrysalis." These poofy wool cocoonlike shapes can be textural and as colorful as you want them to be. In making this yarn, you are essentially spinning the core portion and the wrapping portion at the same time.

you will need:

* Fiber for the core (shown here, a solid-color batt)
* Fiber for the "chrysalis" (shown here, multicolored top)

For this technique, I use a batt for the core yarn and hand-painted top for wrapping. Begin by predrafting both the core and the chrysalis fiber. Spin a length of core fiber, just enough to ensure sufficient twist to hold the yarn together. From now on this will be known as your "base yarn" and it will act the same way as the singles or thread used in traditional core spinning.

Firmly grip the point of twist to stop it from traveling up into your fiber supply. Especially at first, you may need to slow down or even stop treadling at this point to prevent overtwisting and corkscrews in your yarn. In the same hand, hold the cocoon fiber just above the point of twist (between the orifice and the twist-controlling hand). Simultaneously

let go of your tight pinch at the point of twist, resume a normal tension with your twist-regulating fingers, return to your former treadling speed (if you slowed down), and allow the newly introduced fiber to be grabbed by the twist of your base yarn.

Continue to draft the base yarn while holding the wrapping fiber and allowing it to twist around the base yarn. This loosely held section creates the poofy texture. When the wrapping fiber is almost entirely used up, finish the section by bringing the end up toward the wheel and allowing it to be firmly anchored by the twist.

To create more dramatic wool chrysalides, simply draft your wrapping fiber thicker. Once your fingers are adept at these actions, you can create slubs within the wool cocoons by drafting in a thick-and-thin style (see page 56).

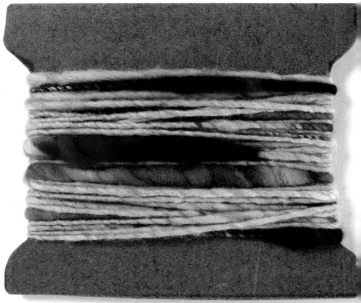

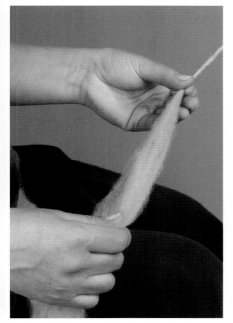

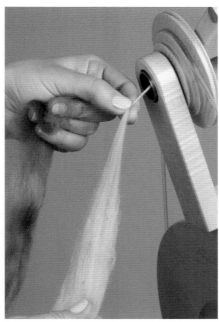

1. Attach the core fiber to the leader and spin a short length to establish the twist.

2. Pinch the point of twist firmly.

3. Hold the wrapping fiber above the point of twist, relax your pinching hand, and resume your normal treadling speed.

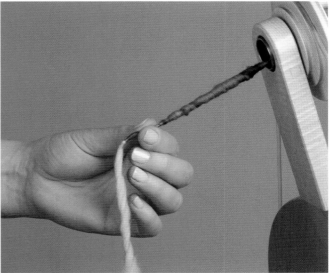

5. When the piece of wrapping fiber is near the end, hold it toward the orifice and allow the twist to capture it.

4. Draft the base yarn with your right hand and hold the wrapping fiber loosely to the left, allowing it to cover the base and puff up.

Coils

Coiling is a plying technique that produces a very sculptural yarn. This approach can be used sparingly or to the extreme to add excitement to your yarn. Like core spinning, it involves adding elements to an already-spun base yarn, but because the outside layer is already-spun singles, it's considered a plying technique. Make the singles as wild or tame as you like; even when made with plain singles, coils are irresistible.

you will need:

* Core thread
* Lots of prespun singles

coil materials

Being a plying technique, spinning coils requires two yarns: a core or binder (which will be partly or mostly hidden) and a wrapping yarn. Making effective coils is at least a two-step process: spinning the singles, then spinning the coils.

You will need a lot of high-twist singles; it takes roughly 100 yards (91 m) to make 10 yards (9 m) of tightly coiled yarn. (This will vary depending on the thickness of your singles and how tightly or sparingly you make your coils.) I prefer to spin the singles for the wrapping yarn worsted-style, but see what works best for you. Choose from top, batts, or even uncarded fiber—any fiber that will respond well to being spun with high twist. You can even spin a highly textured singles with art yarn techniques, then multiply the effect by making it into coils, or spin extremely thick-and-thin singles to make a yarn that looks almost beaded.

When spinning singles for coiling, you will need to work against your spinning habits and add more twist than you normally would. The singles should have almost twice as many twists per inch as for a balanced plied yarn—not so much that the yarn makes corkscrews, but enough to stay together while being plied at a dramatic angle.

When you select your binder, keep in mind the kind of coiled yarn you want to make. First and foremost, you need to choose something strong and smooth. Your singles need to be able to slide up the binder; anything too coarse will be a challenge. For densely packed coils, crochet cotton is ideal; if you plan on using coils sparingly, the binder will show. I like using high-twist singles with some nylon content for added strength. Combinations of wooly nylon (stretchy serger thread) and rayon threads work, too; these come in various colors, including metallic, and are available in most sewing stores. You can even try using some of the more novel commercial yarns—try eyelash! With a bit of experimentation you will find what fits your style best.

ready to coil

I wind the singles into a center-pull ball and keep it on my lap, then place the binder on a lazy kate behind and to the left of me. This helps me maintain control of the parts while holding the singles at the best angle to wind onto the binder. Play with your positioning; it will vary depending on which hand you favor, your height, and your posture.

Secure your binder thread to the wrapping singles by tying a knot—not the most attractive, but functional. Then tie them directly to the leader. (This will mean cutting or breaking off the plied yarn from the leader when you are finished, but this method holds up best.)

Treadling at a swift, even pace, hold your binder thread straight and your singles at a 45° angle, allowing it to wrap around the binder. Keep spinning and wrapping until the singles have wound all the way back to the back hand.

Holding the binder taut, push the wraps up toward the orifice; the more you push the wraps together, the less your binder will show. Experiment with pushing the coils very close together, leaving exposed binder thread, and alternating between them.

When you have used up all of your singles or spun as much as you want, push the last of the coils up as firmly as you can, then tie a secure knot. This helps ensure the coils won't slide off the binder when the yarn is removed from the bobbin and washed.

MAKING COILS

1. Hold the binder thread straight and the singles at a 45° angle.

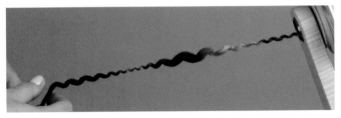

2. Allow the singles to wind on until all the binder in front of your hands is covered.

3. With the hand controlling the singles, push the coils up the binder.

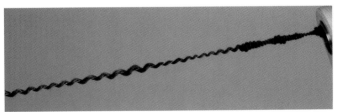

4. If you prefer, the coils can cover only part of the core, leaving part of a decorative binder thread exposed.

5. If the singles was spun thick-and-thin, the coils will look like a string of beads.

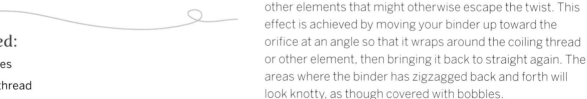

Knopping Coils

Knopping can be used as a decorative element or to add strength to a coiled yarn. Like coils or core spinning, it works by holding two elements at dramatically different angles.

you will need:

* Prespun singles
* A decorative thread

A variation on the coiling technique, knopping can be particularly striking when you are using the coils sparingly with a more decorative thread or a handspun binder. Knopping can also help secure flyaway ends, add-ins, or other elements that might otherwise escape the twist. This effect is achieved by moving your binder up toward the orifice at an angle so that it wraps around the coiling thread or other element, then bringing it back to straight again. The areas where the binder has zigzagged back and forth will look knotty, as though covered with bobbles.

1. To knopp over coils, reverse angles—hold the singles straight and angle the binder toward the orifice.

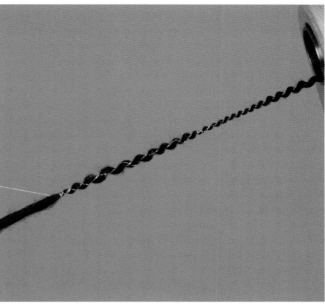

2. Bring the binder back to be nearly straight. Repeat these two steps as much as you like.

3. Knopping over coils adds a layer of color and texture.

4. Pushing up more coils against the knopped portion can create knotty and intriguing bobbles.

add-ins

There are a number of ways to add ornaments such as beads and buttons to art yarns. Envision yarns with pom-poms, charms, wing nuts, washers—almost anything that has (or can be made to have) a hole through it can become part of your yarns. They can be anything you can think of to string, fasten, or otherwise incorporate in your yarn. Practice adding elements by stringing them on one long singles, spinning in short lengths of yarn with attachments, or even breaking the main yarn to put a bead right where you want it.

Plying Beads

The first and most obvious way to add these elements is to thread them directly onto high-twist singles or commercial thread, then secure them by plying with another singles. If you decide to use a commercial thread, choose something decorative, as it will show in your yarn. If you prefer a handspun yarn, make sure it is thin, even, and durable enough to fit through the beads and hold them securely. (Keep in mind that the beads may abrade the yarn, especially if they have sharp edges.)

String all of the beads you plan to use on your thread or singles before you begin plying. Place the plain and beaded yarns on a lazy kate or hold them comfortably and ply normally, gently controlling the twist where the yarns come together. As you treadle, slide the beads up the thread or singles toward the orifice at desired intervals—regularly or randomly, as you prefer. As you continue plying, the twist between the two plies will help encapsulate the bead and hold it in place.

you will need:

* Handspun singles
* Beads (or buttons or other elements)
* Very even handspun binder or decorative thread

PLYING WITH STRUNG BEADS

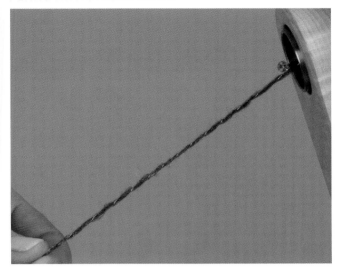

1. Ply your plain singles and beaded thread together normally, controlling the twist gently.

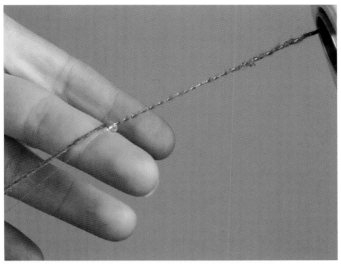

2. When you reach a spot where you would like to place a bead, slide one up toward the orifice into the point of twist.

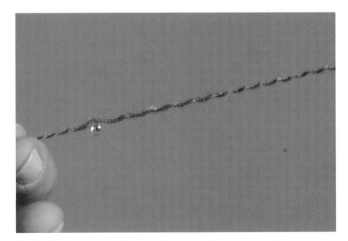

3. Continue to ply, allowing the twist to run over the bead and secure it.

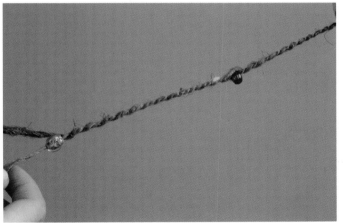

4. If you have threaded the beads on handspun singles, the yarn will probably fill the bead's hole better and keep it in place.

Adding Beads to Singles

Although plying is the most common and easiest way to add beads or other items to yarn, don't despair if you have singles in mind! The following techniques allow you to add beads securely to a yarn without plying.

beads on the spot

One way to add items that is principally useful when making singles as your finished yarn is simply to add a strung bead in a particular spot while spinning. This method also requires prestringing beads on another thread or singles, though you will need to cut or break the stringing yarn between beads. Begin spinning your main singles as usual, then stop the

you will need:

* Prespun singles
* Lengths of thread or yarn prestrung with beads, pom-poms, or other elements

twist with the fingers you usually use to control the drafting triangle. Place the end of a prethreaded string or thread in the center of the drafting triangle, then release the twist and allow it to engulf the thread for a few inches. Continue drafting and spinning the fiber for your main singles while the new thread is incorporated. Just before the twist reaches the bead, gently tug the thread to make sure that it is securely incorporated in the twist. If it remains firmly anchored, proceed with spinning and allow the twist to pass over the bead. If your tug is met with no resistance and the thread begins to pull out, continue spinning the thread with the new singles until you are confident that they

have become firmly incorporated or knopp over the object, encasing it with its own thread. When all the beads have been added, embed the tail of the stringing yarn in the twist and core spin over it, hiding and securing the end.

Securing with knopping is not only a highly effective way to secure an item, but it can also add an exciting point of interest. To knopp an object such as a bead, first allow it to enter the drafting zone, then bring the thread toward the orifice so that it wraps over the bead. Return the beaded thread to its original angle.

BEADS ON THE SPOT

1. Restraining the twist, place one end of the bead-strung thread in the center of the drafting triangle of the main yarn.

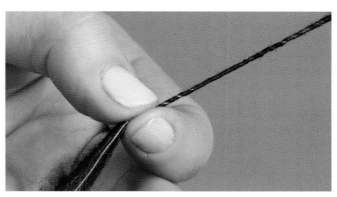

2. Release the twist and hold the fiber and thread together.

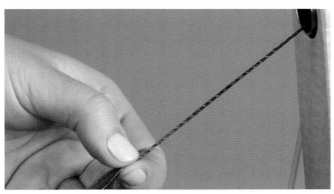

3. Continue drafting the singles while guiding the thread into the drafting triangle.

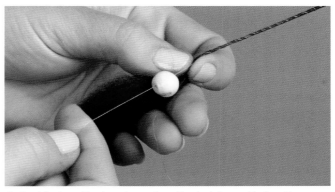

4. Just before the bead reaches the twist, gently tug the beaded thread.

5. If the beaded thread remains secure, allow the twist to run over it.

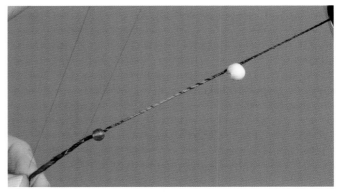

6. If the thread threatens to pull out, use the beaded thread to knopp over the bead.

core-spun additions

Using the techniques of core spinning (see page 72) to attach add-ins is another eye-catching but secure method of creating a beaded yarn. A core thread prestrung with beads (or pom-poms, shown at right) can temporarily become a base for the developing singles. By lifting the core out of the drafting triangle, you bring a bead to the surface. A little loose fiber helps secure the ends in place.

you will need:

* Predrafted fiber
* Lengths of thread or yarn prestrung with beads, pom-poms, or other elements
* Loose fiber (locks or sari silk)

Introduce the embellished thread to the drafting triangle as for on-the-spot beading (see page 88) and continue drafting and spinning until the new thread is secure. Then lift the beaded thread over the fiber at an angle, allowing the new thread to affect the twist and wrap around the developing "base" yarn.

When a bead is approaching the yarn, bring the thread down to a less severe angle while still allowing it to wrap around the forming singles. When the bead reaches the drafting triangle, take some loose fibers and introduce them to the twist, allowing them to grab onto the base yarn and thread. Core spin the loose fibers over the yarn and the thread.

CORE SPINNING BEADS

1. Place the beaded thread in the drafting triangle of the forming singles.

2. Draft the fiber and the thread together until the thread is securely attached.

3. Hold the thread over the base yarn at a 45°–90° angle.

4. Allow the thread to knopp around the forming singles.

5. Reduce the angle and bring the thread closer to the forming singles when a bead is near the twist.

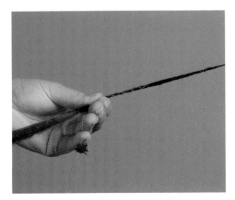

6. Although the twist angle is reduced, the thread will still be wrapping around the forming yarn.

7. Allow the bead into the drafting triangle and at the same time introduce loose fibers to the twist.

8. Core spin the loose fibers around the forming singles to secure the thread.

break for beads

Yet another way to add beads is to add them one at a time while spinning. This technique lets you place a bead right where you want it, avoid prestringing, and add beads directly to a thick-and-thin yarn. However, it is highly time-consuming, because you will need to stop and start, breaking and rejoining the forming yarn for each bead.

Begin by spinning a length of yarn. Stop at the spot where you would like to add a bead, making sure that the ends of your fiber are smooth by pinching the twist. Use your fingers to slide the bead gently up onto the yarn singles, pushing it a few inches toward the orifice. After the bead is in place, allow some of the twist to run out from the end of the broken yarn, which will make it easier to join a new length of fiber and resume spinning. You may decide to tie an overhand knot behind or over the bead, which will secure its position on your yarn.

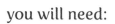

you will need:

* Loose beads
* Predrafted fiber (preferably one that will be easy to break and rejoin)

BREAKING FOR BEADS

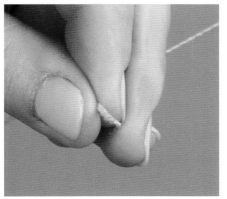

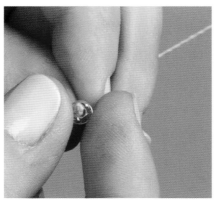

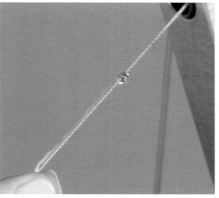

1. When you reach a spot where you'd like to add a bead, break off the fiber source, leaving a smooth end.

2. Gently slide a bead onto the yarn.

3. Slide the bead a few inches up the yarn toward the orifice.

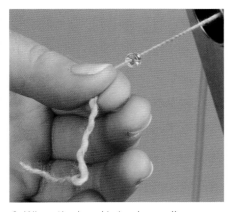

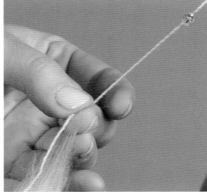

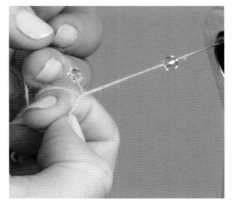

4. When the bead is in place, allow some twist to run out the end of the yarn.

5. Rejoin the fiber source and spin until you'd like to place another bead.

6. If you want to secure the bead in place, you can tie an overhand knot.

7. The knot will keep the bead from slipping back and forth on the yarn.

Adding Cocoons

Creating a near-invisible connection gives the illusion that your object is simply floating on the yarn. Take advantage of wool's cuticle to secure lengths of prespun singles strung with silk cocoons or other dangly items. The cocoons will be attached with a method that is less visible than core spinning or knopping.

you will need:

* ✳ Predrafted fiber in fiber that will felt
* ✳ Tapestry or other large-eye needle
* ✳ Lengths of prespun singles in a fiber that will felt
* ✳ Silk cocoons

Begin by threading the cocoons on the prespun singles. Cut the singles into manageable lengths, about 10" to 11" (25.5 to 28 cm) long. Using a tapestry needle and working from inside the cocoon, poke two or more holes in the bottom of each one (such as a button). Thread the tapestry needle and string each cocoon with one length of singles, passing through both holes to secure it. Tie the ends of the singles in a knot, leaving about 5" (12.5 cm) of tail on each end. As with any preparation, I find it helpful to string all the elements that I will be using ahead of time. This way, I don't need to stop spinning to string up more—the process is time-consuming already.

Predraft the top that you will be using for the main yarn. Attach it to the leader and spin until you've found a rhythm. When you want to add a cocoon, slow down or stop treadling and stop the twist with your twist-regulating hand. (You may want to draft the main fiber ever so slightly thinner to keep the diameter consistent when the cocoon is added.) Open up the fibers in the drafting triangle and insert one end of the prespun singles into the triangle.

Resume a normal treadling pace and use your twist-control finger to quickly move the twist down over the area where the threading singles has been inserted. Hold the top (which is forming your base yarn) parallel to the threaded cocoon, allowing the threading singles to be wrapped in the fibers. Spin until the join feels secure, then give a gentle tug to make sure.

When you reach the end of the threading singles, open up the fibers in the drafting triangle again and tuck the end of the threading single into the center of the triangle. This will hide and secure it.

Choosing Materials for Cocoon Spinning

For this yarn I have used wool top for the base yarn, silkworm cocoons for the embellishment, and handspun high-twist 100% wool singles to secure the cocoons. (Before handling the cocoons, moisturize your hands. As with any other type of silk, cocoons can pull or fray if snagged by dry hands.) Choose prespun singles in a similar or complementary color to the top for the main yarn so that the two will be blended.

To secure the add-ins to the yarn, it is important that wool of the singles not be superwash-treated. With washing and wear, the follicles of the threading singles will adhere to the follicles of the fiber in the base yarn and lock the yarns together even more. (I learned the importance of this the hard way—once I used a single with a high nylon content to thread cocoons and paired it with a 100% wool base yarn. After washing and setting the twist, the wool base shrank slightly, while the threading singles did not. As a result, the cocoons looked a bit floppy, and they did not feel as secure as they could have been.)

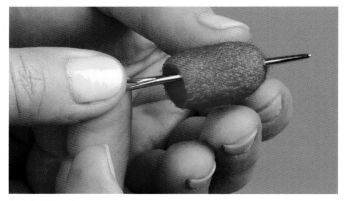

1. Working from the inside of the cocoon, poke at least 2 holes in the end as though for a button.

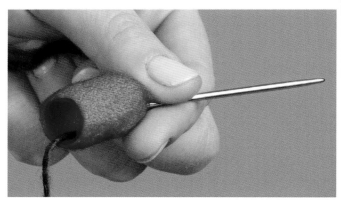

2. With a length of the singles threaded on the tapestry needle, pass through the bottom of the cocoon.

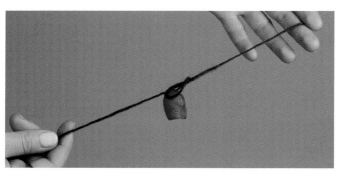

4. Tie a knot with the tails to hold the cocoon in place.

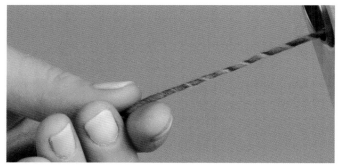

5. Spin to the place where you'd like to insert a cocoon and pinch off the twist.

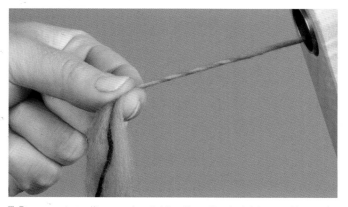

7. Resume treadling and quickly allow the twist to run through the fiber and the singles.

8. Hold the singles together with the fiber, allowing the fiber to wrap around the singles.

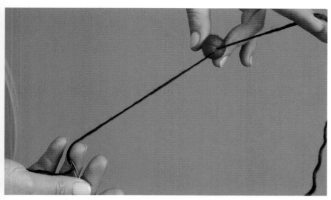

3. Thread the singles through both holes, leaving a 5"
(12.5 cm) tail at each end.

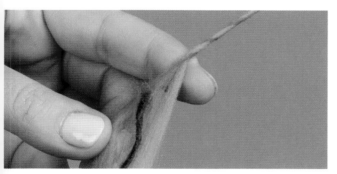

6. Spread the drafting triangle open and place the end of the
singles in the center.

9. When you reach the tail of the singles, bury the end in
the drafting triangle to hide and secure it.

unconventional plying

With all the effort you've put into preparing and spinning singles to express your artistic vision, a nonstandard plying technique may be just the thing to set off your unique yarn—or you may want to make your major statement in the way you combine the yarns in plying. We've touched on some yarns that use plying techniques, such as adding beads with a second yarn or coiling, but the techniques below rely on using both plies as equals rather than one hiding or accenting the other. You can experiment with using these techniques for three or more plies, too.

High/low, or Mock Bouclé

Although traditional bouclé yarn is a somewhat complex novelty structure, we can create a yarn with the characteristic uneven, knobby surface by making a two-ply yarn composed of one larger-diameter singles spun at a lower twist angle and one smaller-diameter singles spun at a higher twist angle.

you will need:

* Thick low-twist singles
* Thin high-twist singles

To make this yarn successfully, you will need to be comfortable producing a sturdy, stable, thin high-twist singles as well as a thicker but still stable low-twist single—thus the name "high/low." Aside from adding texture, the high/low effect will distribute your color in a subtle and interesting way. Being able to create a good blend (see "Blend Fiber & Color," page 36) is helpful, although not necessary; with a blend you can expand your palette and incorporate just the right amount of whimsy (nylon sparkle or silk sari) or seriousness (rare-breed wool or hemp) to your yarn. You can even employ color-shifting methods (see An Exercise in Color, page 44) to make one multicolored singles to be plied with a solid.

Begin by setting up to make a two-ply as you feel most comfortable, whether on a lazy kate or from center-pull balls. Attach both singles to your leader. If you've spun spiral yarns before, you might put more tension on the larger singles. Try your best to ignore that impulse and keep the tension even, allowing the plies to fall where they may. If you feel that the finished yarn is plied too loosely for your liking, you can always run it back through the wheel, adding more twist in the plying direction. Before you do, though, remember that after finishing the plies will adhere more to each other; washing, shocking, and whacking the yarn makes the follicles expand and the fibers bloom.

To take this technique a step further, add more tension on the higher-twist singles. This will enhance the uneven texture; with even more tension, you produce a slightly coiled yarn. With experimentation you can find the exact combination of texture, color, and distribution of each that you are seeking.

PLYING HIGH/LOW FOR MOCK BOUCLÉ

1. Set up for a two-ply yarn, but hold one ply in each hand to control them individually.

2. Holding the thin singles under tighter tension can make the thicker singles puff up almost to the point of a semi-coiled yarn.

Worms

Another plying technique, which can be combined with high/low plying or done with matching singles, is to ply "worms." (Yes, you can make your yarn into worms, on purpose.) It creates a different texture, similar to a commercial eyelash, with lots of drama for shockingly little effort.

you will need:

* Two sets of singles for plying

Set up to spin a two-ply using your preferred method and ply until you reach a section where you want to add an eyelash or worm. Just below your twist-control fingers (where the two singles are not twisted together), gently lift a section of singles away from the other ply (which remains under tension) and loop it around your finger. Hold one end with your left hand and pinch the other end with your right hand, then release. This creates a length of singles with a mini self-ply, or what we are calling worms. Repeat at intervals as desired. (If you do this consistently with only one of your singles, you will need extra yardage of that yarn.)

PLY WORMS

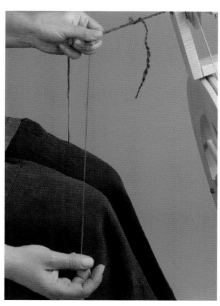

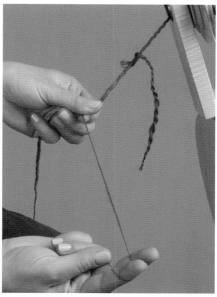

1. Spin a two-ply yarn until you reach a point where you would like to add a worm or an eyelash.

2. Hold one of the singles away from the other.

3. Gently loop that singles around your finger.

4. Hold both ends of that section in your left hand and pull the loop taut with your right.

5. When you release the loop, the doubled strand plies back on itself and creates a worm.

Tie-ins

To get a more extreme eyelash effect, you can physically tie in yarn or other elements as you ply. This makes for a lot of stop-and-start action, but you can place additional elements exactly where you want them. Tied-in items can dangle away from the yarn or hug it tightly.

you will need:

* Two (or more) sets of singles for plying
* Yarn or thread to tie on (may be strung with beads or other items)

Cut the yarn or thread that you plan to tie on into pieces a few inches long, then set up to ply as usual. When you want to add a new element, stop plying for a moment and keep the singles under tension. Loop a strand of cut yarn around one of the plies and tie it in a secure knot or bow. This is a fairly time-consuming process, but you can add some highly interesting objects with your cut bits. Additionally, the knot helps keep the added element in place firmly, a particular benefit when working with slippery elements, fabric, or plastic.

TYING IN ELEMENTS

1. Ply until you reach a place where you would like to tie in a new element.

2. Select a piece of yarn or an element you'd like to tie in and hold it perpendicular to one of the plies.

3. Tie an overhand knot with the tie-in element to hold it securely.

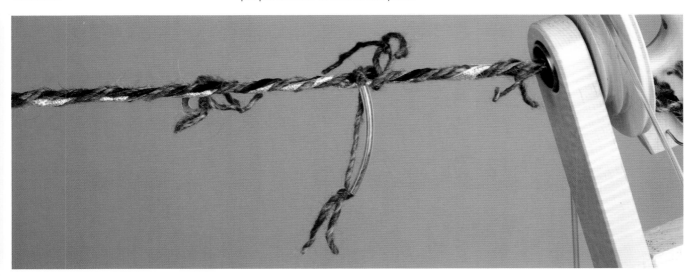

4. By tying in other elements, you can add rich textures to your yarn.

Plying in Locks

Instead of adding locks in singles (see page 64), you can create yarn with unspun elements when plying. The twist that holds the plies together can capture additional fiber and hold it firmly; instead of locks, try sari silk, lengths of yarn, or other items.

you will need:

* Two (or more) sets of singles for plying
* Clean dyed locks, sari silk, or other loose fiber

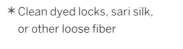

Set up your bobbins of singles and begin to ply as usual. When you find a place where you'd like to add a lock, hold the plies apart. Pinch off the twist and open up the drafting triangle. Place the cut end of the lock between the plies and hold it in the twist zone. Allow the plying twist to grab the cut ends to secure the lock in the yarn. When the end of the lock is firmly attached, hold the remaining fiber out of the twist and let it go once the twist is well past it. Finishing the yarn with a warm wash and a good thwack will help secure the locks between the plies.

INSERTING LOCKS WHILE PLYING

1. Hold the plies apart and place the cut end of the lock in the twist zone.

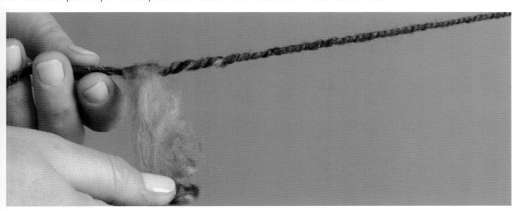

2. Once the lock is secure, hold most of the fiber out of the twist.

3. After the plying twist has moved through the lock area, let go of the lock and resume plying normally.

unspinnables

Spinning fabric, plastic shopping bags, or other nontraditional materials isn't as difficult as it may sound. True, they don't really draft, but so what? They spin. Look beyond traditional fiber sources and start imagining new uses for all kinds of material— paper, cassette tape, vines, police tape, anything that can hold twist.

Fabric

Fabric yarn is a great way to recycle old clothing. See a terrific vintage dress at the thrift store for fifty cents that is (of course) three sizes too small? Spin it! In the vein of the memory quilts that have become increasingly popular over the years, I decided to make a memory yarn from some of my daughter's old dresses (which may be knitted into a memory purse if she has her way).

you will need:

* Fabric, cut into long strips
* Prespun singles or thread

Begin by taking a section of the fabric and cutting around the perimeter in an almost circular manner, turning corners until you reach the center. You should end up with one continuous strip of fabric.

Because fabric doesn't draft like fiber does, I use an overhand knot to tie the beginning to my leader, an easy way to make sure it is secure. Gently treadle and allow the strips to slide through your fingers, experimenting with the tension and ratio until you're happy with the singles. Once you have an even rhythm, the twist virtually takes care of itself, and like magic, nicely stable singles emerge from strips of fabric.

Adding new strips of fabric can be a bit tricky, because there are no small singular fibers to adhere to one another. I've found it necessary to open up the twist a bit and insert the beginning of a new strip inside the drafting triangle when the old strip is done. After a small length has been spun, the fabric becomes twisted, or folded in a round way; open up that fold and place the new strip inside. Using prespun singles or thread to knopp over the join can also help secure new strips of fabric or other elements.

If you're tired of a particular section of fabric or you come across a spot you don't like, simply snip the end and add in a new strip. If the starting fabric or garment has some unusual elements such as ruffles, trim, or stitching, it can create its own textural section.

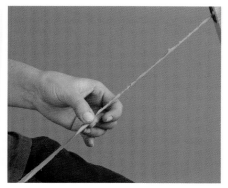

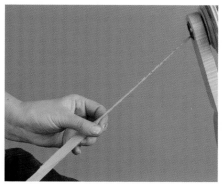

1. Begin to treadle gently, seeking a comfortable rhythm and amount of twist.

2. The twist smooths the fabric into an even singles.

3. To add a new strip of fabric, a length of yarn, or another element, hold the fabric in the drafting triangle open and insert the new element.

4. To change strips, just snip off the end of the current one and join a new strip.

5. Using a length of prespun singles to knopp over joins can help secure the fabric.

6. Knopping also adds a purely decorative element.

7. A ruffle from the original dress adds texture and dimension to the yarn.

Plastic Bags

Spinning the pile of plastic shopping bags you have stashed under your kitchen sink—you know, the ones that multiply when you aren't looking—is very similar to spinning fabric. Tie your bobbin's leader directly onto the plastic bag and go! There are a few special considerations when spinning the slippery plastic material.

you will need:

* Plastic bags
* Prespun yarn or commercial thread

Begin by cutting plastic bags into strips. Depending on the effect you're after, choose bags of all one color or a whole rainbow. Newspaper delivery bags can be especially colorful. Cut deliberate ruffles or shaggy pieces to vary the texture from smooth to frilly.

Because plastic bags are slippery, you may want to add some stability by knopping the length of your yarn with another yarn or commercial thread (here, a commercial thread with some novelty elements was used). This can also add some color to what might otherwise be a monochromatic yarn. Tie the binder thread and plastic bags to the leader and spin them together, knopping the thread up and down the plastic portions. Join new pieces of plastic bag by pinching off the twist and inserting a new piece between the old plastic and the binder thread. Knopp the thread over the join to secure both ends.

SPINNING PLASTIC BAGS

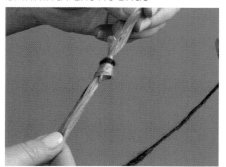

1. Tie a strip of plastic bag to your leader with an overhand knot.

2. Hold the plastic and thread in separate hands to adjust the tension individually, allowing the thread to wrap around the plastic.

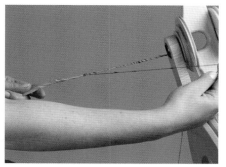

3. Bring the yarn or thread closer to the orifice to knopp over areas that have already been spun.

4. To join a new plastic strip, pinch off the twist and hold the thread and old plastic bag apart.

5. Insert the new plastic strip between the old one and the thread.

6. Slowly allow the twist into all three components, making sure that all of them are captured in the twist.

7. Allow the thread to wrap around the join, knopping to secure it.

8. When both plastic pieces are secure, allowing a small piece to be free from the twist can create a decorative, ruffle-like element.

artistic inspiration

COMBINING TECHNIQUES

Now that you have the tools to make art yarns, the direction that you take them in is up to you. You can start with materials that spark your interest, a person who inspires you, a concept to explore—almost anything can be the seed for creating art in yarn.

To look for your own inspirations, take a camera out into the world and snap a few photos. Take these photos with you to four different stores: a thrift store, a fabric/notions store, a hardware store, and of course your local fiber store. Examine the sky, buildings, people, flora, and fauna. Look for these elements (or items that represent these elements) at all four stores.

Here are a few yarns I made using a variety of the techniques demonstrated in this book. All of the elements were chosen with intention, producing what I consider an art yarn.

Left-handed Monkey Wrench

This yarn came about by simply being itself. It was inspired by thin coppery singles that I blended and spun—even though the singles may be the least noticeable thing about this yarn. When I went down the aisles of the hardware store, the coppery findings begged to be spun with that yarn. In stringing my hardware "beads," I realized that they overwhelmed the delicate-looking singles. I added dyed wool top for balance; the eye is drawn to large sections of color or slubs, making the brassy bits an element of the yarn rather than the whole focus.

The singles were spun clockwise, so I held them side by side with the top and added counterclockwise (plying) twist. I drafted the top as for a bulky thick-and-thin yarn to create body and drama. Drafting and spinning this way created the "high-low" effect of a high-twist yarn paired with a lower-twist yarn. The hardware was incorporated as it came into the drafting zone, sometimes sparingly before or after slubs, and other times more liberally.

materials used:

* Handpainted wool top
* Thin singles
* Brass-colored hardware (bushings, bolts, etc.)

techniques used:

* Blending fibers (see page 41)
* High-twist singles (see page52)
* Spinning thick-and-thin yarn (see page 56)
* Plying beads (see page 86)

In and Out of the Garden

Cucumbers and morning glories growing in my garden were on my mind during a fun trip to the fabric store. The multicolored blue, green, yellow, and purple thick-and-thin singles represent air, water, sun, earth, and the life growing in the garden. I began by plying it with a purple ribbon and purple mesh. The ribbon evokes the plants' tendrils; the netting stands for the fences and other physical barriers that protect gardens. I added caterpillars of green fuzzy trim secured by knopping with tendrils of purple ribbon. The large and lush green leaves are represented by core-spun green locks alternated with ribbon. The finishing touch was the worms, added for the obvious reason: we all want worms in our gardens.

materials used:

* Multicolored thick-and-thin yarn
* Green dyed longwool locks
* Purple ribbon
* Purple 1" (2.5 cm) wide mesh
* Fuzzy lime-green trim

techniques used:

* Spinning thick-and-thin yarn (see page 56)
* Core spinning (see page 74)
* Knopping (see page 82)
* Plying worms (see page 102)
* Plying in locks (see page 106)
* Spinning fabric (see page 110)

Bella Yarn

Finding the inspiration for this yarn was not difficult—it was handed to me. My daughter has outgrown some old sundresses, and instead of donating them to the thrift store, I put them with my craft supplies. I had intended to make her a memory quilt, but the opportunity arose to create a yarn from them. My daughter saw me cutting up her old dresses into strips, and she objected until I told her I would create something for her. Talk about pressure! Pleasing a seven-year-old girl is no easy task.

I chose accoutrements that reminded me of her qualities: The cotton strips cut from her dress are her strengths, and ribbon bows show her sweetness. The brown ribbon roughly tied in with edges poking out is her rough-and-tumble side, and the fabric rosettes show her ability to love. The completed yarn is a tangible reminder of the growth and evolution of my daughter—the way one stage replaces another and nothing ever remains the same.

materials used:

* Strips of fabric
* Three colors of ribbon
* Fabric rosebuds

techniques used:

* Spinning fabric (see page 110)
* Tie-ins (see page 104)

Industrial

Each element in this yarn represents something I see or feel in a photograph I took of a cityscape. I chose the gray wool singles to represent the unseen people, then plied it with a stiff black suede cording to indicate what keeps people tethered to the city. I added flashy beads strung on a metallic thread, evoking the creative elements of the city.

The sparkling silver and white pom-poms represent stars—the dreams we aspire to wherever we live—and the silver ribbon suggests electricity. The gray wool tie-ins symbolize the sheer number of people in cities, often living and working one on top of another. The metal washers are the steel skyscrapers and the metal of cars and buses. The tied-in plastic tubing represents the masks we sometimes wear to protect ourselves from other people. Once I had all of the elements, I cabled the yarn, representing the many seen and unseen layers of the city.

materials used:

* Gray handspun singles
* Black suede cording
* Pom-poms and blue retro-reflective beads
* Silver and blue metallic threads
* Silver ribbon
* Silver-colored hardware
* Lengths of clear plastic tubing
* Metal springs

techniques used:

* Blending fibers (see page 41)
* Plying beads (see page 86)
* Tie-ins (see page 104)

resources

Buffalo Gold
buffalogold.net
bison

Dharma Trading
dharmatrading.com
Jacquard acid dyes

R.H. Lindsay Company
rhlindsaywool.com
wool top

Spunky Eclectic
spunkyeclectic.com
glitz, hemp

Still River Mill
stillrivermill.com
locks, wool, and fleece processing

index